D03892I5

KARL MARX

His Life and Teachings

KARL MARX

His Life and Teachings

(Leben und Lehre)

by

FERDINAND TÖNNIES

translated from the German by
CHARLES P. LOOMIS
and
INGEBORG PAULUS

THE MICHIGAN STATE UNIVERSITY PRESS

1974

Copyright © 1974
The Michigan State University Press
ISBN: 0–87013–181–8
Library of Congress Catalog Card Number: 73–91768

★
  ★
 ★
  ★
   ★

MANUFACTURED IN THE UNITED STATES OF AMERICA

Dedicated to my time-honored friend, the philosopher, social researcher, and social politician, the champion of the workers' cooperative movement, Franz Staudinger, as a late gift for his seventieth birthday, 15 February, 1919.

Contents

Foreword

Tönnies book on *Marx—His Life and Teachings* was published in 1921, thirty-four years after his magnum opus, *Community and Society—Gemeinschaft und Gesellschaft*. In looking back on his own work, he notes in the 1921 book on Marx that *Community and Society* had been deeply influenced by Marx's writings. He relates that he had been a serious Marxian student for forty-two years at the time he capped this interest by writing the 1921 work on Marx. The slimness of the volume —only 148 pages in the original edition—when thought of in relation to the magnitude of Marx's writings, testifies to the highly compressed style and tightly packed thought employed by Tönnies. These features may well explain why there has been no second edition of the work and no English translation. Despite the difficulties of compressed content which are heightened by the process of translation, we believe that the rewards to the English-speaking student of Marx, as well as to the serious general reader, will be great. We know of no sociologist who has demonstrated such detailed knowledge of Marx's writing and who has been able to compress the main themes of Marx in so few pages.

An intimate knowledge of *Capital* is required to enable Tönnies to declare, for example, that nowhere in that three-volume work does the phrase "dictatorship of the proletariat" appear. In a similar vein he is able to say unequivocally that in the forty-year correspondence between Marx and Engels, which occupies four volumes, not once did either of them mention "the materialistic conception of history." The detailed and purposeful reading which underlies such observations is here available to the English reader for the first time. What Tönnies has done is no mere rehash of well-known Marxian concepts. He looked for specific ideas, apparently in an effort to sort out what was truly Marxian from what is Marxian only by imputation. Thus, although Tönnies gives major attention in the book to what he thought was Marx's chief contribution—namely, his *Critique of the Political Economy*—he also discusses other themes. For example, he reviews the much-debated subject of Marx's effort to free his mode of thinking from that of Hegel and likewise criticizes Marx's treatment of morality, particularly that of the worker, as mere epiphenomenon.

Although Tönnies prepared the present volume for the general reader, his own sociological orientation is clearly present. Marx's place in conflict theory, for example, is duly noted and supported by the famous observation "no antagonism, no progress." Tönnies' sociological approach is observable, however, as he criticizes Marx on the grounds of evidence that all conflicts and contradictions are not resolvable by revolution or other means: that societies can be irreparably damaged if subjected solely to change wrought by conflict. In our view, Tönnies correctly questions Marx's "certainty about the decline of the present and the rise of the future." In this connection, he calls into question Marx's use of the analogy of the transition from feudalism to capitalism as a model for predicting the future.

Tönnies credits Marx with providing the first and best analysis of capitalism but notes that whereas Marx gives the industrialist the highest priority in originating and maintaining capitalism, he himself would give the merchant or trader the crucial role. To our knowledge, no sociologist has pointed out as effectively as has Tönnies the disrespect and disparagement Marx had for the huckster, or *Schacher*, and his activity. Both Marx and Engels considered the bargaining activity of the huckster, or trader, as a most despicable core aspect of capitalism. We are tempted to ask whether or not this evaluation of bargaining and trading in Marxian thinking has anything to do with the relative frequency with which noncommunists, at what they believe to be a conference or bargaining table, are confronted with negation from their rivals, the communists.

Tönnies, of course, notes as a basic contribution of Marx to sociology the stress placed on stratification but he also cites Marx's recognition that organizational ability and activity are important inputs in the productive process. Nonetheless, he is not persuaded that Marx's basic insights led him to viable conclusions concerning the sociological and economic aspects of

leadership and management. A case in point is Marx's example
of the hundred men hired by the entrepreneur. The manager
can structure the work situation so that the men are working
uncooperatively as individual workers, or he can encourage an
amount of teamwork which will yield satisfaction to the workers as well as a relatively greater production with lower ex-
penditure of energy. Tönnies criticizes Marx's uncertainty and
ambiguity in his treatment of this entrepreneural input. He
views Marx's refusal to attach value to the functions of management and supervision as unrealistic, charging that in this Marx
is influenced by his *a priori* conclusion that capital and labor
are always separated and antagonistic and that the former
contains management and always exploits the latter.

Tönnies praises Marx's explanations of the development of
the factory system from its predecessors but criticizes him for
failing to use the dialectic method in explaining its origin.
According to Tönnies, had Marx studied the development of
some craft and guild organizations and family enterprises such
as peasant farms historically and dialectically as they were
changing into huge rational organizations he would not have
credited certain producers, including master craftsmen, guild
and craft leaders, with so much of the innovation. The trader
with his *Gesellschaft-like* mentality is the actor whom Tönnies
credits as being most responsible for bringing the factory system and rational bureaucracy into existence. The master
craftsman and other leaders in the crafts and guilds, Tönnies
points out, usually enjoyed Gemeinschaft-like relationships
with artisans and understudies. The relations between such
actors and their subordinates could rarely be viewed as mere
means to ends as is necessary in rational bureaucracy. The
Gesellschaft-like trader, on the other hand, entertained exactly the same sentiments for junk and old rags which he was
buying and selling as he did for the talents of great artists and
musicians whom he might be promoting. Whereas Marx emo-
tionally declared that only by eliminating capitalism can society free itself and at the same time eliminate the huckster
and the *Schacher,* Tönnies sees in this latter figure the primary
agent in the development and maintenance of modern rational organization and capitalism.

Tönnies calls attention to the insightful manner in which Marx recommended that the work arena in the factory be used in enrichment and development of the personalities of the workers. Both Marx and Tönnies saw this as important long before the socializing influence of the factory became a common theme in the literature on developing countries and before communist countries made it a part of their plans and action.

Tönnies had mastered the more humanistic writings of Marx. He believed that Marx wanted, when possible, to solve the world's problems through democratic action, cooperatives, and legislation rather than through destruction by revolution. He excuses Marx for raging and ranting impatiently against capitalism and its philistines, saying that the mistreatment dealt this genius by society naturally brought about these outbursts.

The foregoing may illustrate what is ahead for the patient reader of *Marx—His Life and Teachings*. We ourselves have profited greatly as we have tried to bring the work to the English reader, and we are grateful to the many who have made the translation possible. Space will not permit us to mention all. We wish to acknowledge the assistance of Professor Rudolf Heberle, who went through Part I up to Chapter 3 of the translation. We owe a special debt to Mrs. Marianne Krull, whose skill as a translator together with her background in sociology was invaluable. Mr. Douglas Parrish, who helped edit the manuscript, and Miss Loraine E. Anderson who, in addition to editorial work, checked the various quotations from English versions of the writings by Marx which were quoted by Tönnies in the German, receive our thanks. Tönnies quoted Marx's German works frequently but included very few citations. The senior translator located most of the quotations and compiled the "Notes and References." He assumed this responsibility and is the one who must be faulted for omissions.

Charles P. Loomis
Ingeborg Paulus

Preface

The literature on Marx[1] especially if articles and essays in journals and newspapers in all languages are considered, is so abundant that it would take a young man a lifetime to master. When a writer thinks of adding another book to this, he may feel called upon to justify himself. Such a justification is not difficult, since it still seems appropriate to present to a learned and knowledge-seeking public another monograph that combines the important facts about the famous man himself as well as some of the chief aspects of his thinking, which in the past, as in the present, has had a profound impact on the moral world.

As is well known, a biography of Marx was published by Franz Mehring a few years ago. This comprehensive work also contained a detailed analysis of Marx's works. However, the material at hand was so voluminous that Mehring felt impelled to add "shortened by the second half" to the customary subheading for his biography, *History of His Life and His Writings* (Preface, p. vii). It is not my intention to compete with this book. I gratefully acknowledge the contribution it has made to my own efforts, and in the present text I frequently refer to it by the notation Mehring.[2] Whoever wishes to dedicate himself to attaining an understanding of Marx the man and his works must diligently study Mehring's biography. However, one must not fail to note, of course, the discrepancies of the epigones,[3] which are of literary as well as political significance, and which also refer to questions of Marx's personality. Mehring, who in earlier years wrote against Treitschke's attacks on socialism, later described social democracy from a national liberal viewpoint. He finally became an intimate friend of Rosa Luxemburg and Karl Liebknecht. His literary executor, who published the second edition of the Marx biography, was sure that Mehring died "on the death" of his friends [Luxemburg and Liebknecht] and that the socialist government of Ebert-Scheidemann-Noske murdered him. On reading Mehring's book one cannot find that this Spartacist trait colored it much.

However, it is indeed the writing of a passionate communist who is eager to protect the anarchist Bakunin, as well as Lassalle, from the hostile criticisms that Marx directed against them.

The present treatise does not consider controversies of this nature because it is limited to the essentials. Neither will an attempt be made to supersede the attractive, but not always accurate, book written by the American, John Spargo, *Karl Marx, Leben und Werk (Life and Work,* authorized German edition, Leipzig, 1912). Spargo's book contains 345 pages, and Mehring's has 544. Spargo also writes as a party member, but his viewpoint differs greatly from Mehring's. Mehring calls Spargo's book a worthless compilation—surely an unjust evaluation. Not until after Mehring's death was the first volume published on Friedrich Engel's biography by Gustav Mayer, *F. E., in seiner Fruhzeit, 1820–1851 (F. E. His Early Years, 1820–1851,* Berlin, Julius Springer, 1920). This extraordinarily rich, critically incisive work seems to create a great literary monument for Marx even earlier than it did for Engels, the main hero of the biography, to whom Marx always deferred. (I have cited this first volume in my text under Mayer.)

Compared with works of this type, the present short monograph can and will advance only modest claims. It is meant mainly for readers who are unable or unwilling to spend the time and effort required by the difficulties of studying Marx's works and those of his biographers and critics. Both Wilbrandt[4] and Beer[5] have set similar goals for themselves, but I believe we can safely exist side by side and that some individuals who read all three monographs will find that they supplement one another. However, I do not want to forestall any judgment. Wilbrandt calls his writing "an attempt at introduction." I prefer to call mine an attempt at presentation and evaluation. More than Wilbrandt did, I shall limit myself to a simple narration of Marx's life and to an explanation of his teachings. A critique, as such, is to be found only at the end of this book. Nevertheless, I expect that just as the reader of Wilbrandt's book is confronted with Marx as well as with Wilbrandt himself, I too shall make myself heard in this present monograph. For forty-two years I have tried to understand Marx and to

learn from him without forfeiting my own independent thinking. The same can be said for Beer's small book, which was
unknown to me until after my book was completed. It is even
shorter than mine, and the viewpoints are somewhat different.[6]

I have tried to remain as independent as possible of all writings here named and all critiques known to me, especially
those of Sombart, Tugan-Baranowsky, and Masaryk. I have
relied on the sources—that is, Marx's own writings—from
which one can also learn the most important facts of his personal development. I can therefore recommend what I offer as
a faithful report by an author who, so to speak, stands behind
his subject. In 1887 in my preface to the first edition of *Community and Society (Gemeinschaft und Gesellschaft)*[7]—
which was subtitled "Essay on Communism and Socialism as
Empirical Forms of Culture"—I emphasized that "my views
had been most thoroughly influenced in a motivating, informa-
tive, and confirming manner by quite different works of three
outstanding authors: namely, the works of Sir Henry Maine, O.
Gierke, and of the most remarkable and most profound social
philosopher, Karl Marx, whose views on economics were most
important for me." At that time I characterized him as the
discoverer of the capitalistic mode of production and as a
thinker who had attempted to give expression to the same idea
which I myself had then wanted to express in my own new
conceptualization. In various instances I referred to Marx's
great accomplishments in the text of that book. For this reason,
Schaeffle, in a recent review of my book, found me guilty of
"not a slight dosage of Marxomania." This was absolutely un-
founded and hardly based on a purely objective viewpoint. I
have never suffered from this passion. Just remembering the
textual references in which the name of Marx was used should
have protected me from this charge. I also cited Comte, Spen-
cer, Schaeffle, and Wagner as authors important to the growth
of my thought; Schaeffle, too, although not in first place.

Since that time I cannot say that I have increased or changed
my knowledge enough to alter considerably my judgment of
Marx and of his significance. Of course, I could not then foresee
how much Marx's thoughts were to inflame and confound im-

mature minds, despite the pains he took and the pride he set in "definitely overcoming the utopian fantasy" (as I expressed myself then). Neither could I foresee how much the passion and confusion of Marx's youth was left in his own thinking, even though his mind was most definitely and rigorously dedicated to knowledge.

FERDINAND TONNIES

NOTES AND REFERENCES

Translators' Note: All notes and references not included in the original Tönnies' manuscripts are preceded by T.N., which stands for Translators' Note.

1. The bibliography on Marx, *Ein Lebensbild Karl Marx in biographisch-bibliographischen Daten (The Life of Karl Marx in Biographical and Bibliographical Data)* by Ernst Drahn (Deutsche Verlagsgesellschaft für Politik und Geschichte m.b.H., 1920, 59 pp.) is important because it lists many widely scattered small essays, newspaper articles, etc., as well as editions of letters and some (but of course not all existing) single letters. However, Sections IV and V, "Bibliography of the Marx Literature" are fragmentary and surpassed by earlier publications.

2. T.N.: Tönnies used the symbol Mg— with the page reference. We have used the whole name but otherwise followed Tönnies' practice of footnoting. Also standard references to quoted portions are noted in the text following Tönnies' custom. When the translators could easily enter citations for quotations, this has been done even when Tönnies used quotation marks without giving the source. The first time a given publication is cited the complete reference is given. Here are some examples: *Capital,* translated from the fourth German edition by E. Utermann (New York: The Modern Library, Random House, 1906), Vol. I, pp. 19-20 is abbreviated to Cap I 19-20; Marx and Engels, *Selected Works* (Moscow: Foreign Languages Publishing House, 1962), Vol. 1, p. 65 is shortened to S W I 65.

3. T.N.: Epigones—less distinguished followers or imitators.

4. Wilbrandt, *Karl Marx (Aus Natur und Geisteswelt) (His Nature and Intellectual World),* Leipzig, 1918.

5. Beer, Karl Marx, *Sein Leben und seine Lehre (His Life and Teachings),* Berlin, 1919.

6. I purposely avoided a discussion with the Marx-critique. I intend to deal with some of the more important critics and commentators (Engels, Kautsky, Bernstein, Mehring, Masaryk, Sombart, Vorlaender, Schulze-Gaevernitz, Tugan, Staudinger, Plenge, Cunow, and others) in a special book on Marxism.

7. T.N.: Eighth revised edition (Leipzig: Hans Buske Verlag, 1935). Translated into English by Charles P. Loomis as *Community and Society—Gemeinschaft und Gesellschaft* (East Lansing, Mich.: Michigan State University Press, 1957; also New York and London: Harper and Row). For a discussion of how these concepts may be used in an analysis of pluralities and change, see Charles P. Loomis's *Social Systems—Essays on Their Persistence and Change* (Princeton, N. J.: S. Van Nostrand, 1965), p. 57 ff.

The sentence expressed in the *Communist Manifesto* by Karl Marx, that the history of society so far is the history of class struggle, throws together two fundamentally different kinds of struggle.

F. Staudinger

PART I

His Life

Chapter 1

UP TO HIS OPTING FOR COMMUNISM AND HIS MEETING WITH FRIEDRICH ENGELS (1818–1843)

Marx's life falls into four clearly distinct parts. The first includes his youth up to his friendship with Engels and his decision to become a communist (1818–1843). The second embraces the period of storm and stress, which lasted until he took domicile in England (1843–1849).[1] The third ends with the publishing of his epoch-making work, *Das Kapital*, Volume 1 (1867). And the fourth finishes with his death in 1883.

1.

Heinrich Karl Marx, born in Trier on May 5, 1818, was a precocious boy and young man. His origin and early surroundings were favorable to his intellectual development. His father, a lawyer and free thinker, grew up under the influence of the great revolution and the Napoleonic period, which provided a background in both German and French cultures. As a good Prussian, however, he leaned toward the Hohenzollern dynasty. His mother was warm-hearted and gentle. The family led an unpretentious, bourgeois, well-to-do life. The family's change to Protestant Christianity of the Lutheran denomination meant little in the inner life of the family, even if outwardly it was of great importance; it was particularly remarkable since both spouses came from families of rabbis.

Little is known about Marx as a young pupil. The young Protestant of Jewish blood was probably educated exclusively by Catholic clergymen, certainly producing a thought-stimulating diversity. He seemed to have been a rather outstanding high school student, since he graduated at seventeen. He enrolled as a law student at Bonn University. Most likely,

Marx's father counted on his gifted son's taking over his law practice; perhaps he would also have been pleased with a career for his son in the Prussian civil service. However, Marx was not merely gifted—he was a genius. His interests were manifold, and writing lyrical poetry was his favorite occupation. For all but the dullest student, philosophy was a matter of course, and Hegel's philosophy was still dominant in the thinking of the intellectuals and academicians.

The young Germany [the movement toward a unified nation] was on the rise. Since the July revolution (1830) this political movement had gained momentum, especially in the Rhineland and in Berlin, with the slogan "Constitution, Parliament, Freedom for all." Great expectations engendered by the accession to the crown of the son of Friedrich Wilhelm III [in 1840] were soon dissipated. The German bourgeoisie, rapidly gaining identity, clamored for national unity in a constitutional government. Its bolder elements incorporated some of the demands of the working class, which in England and France was already impetuously voicing its demands. To be sure, this happened without a clear knowledge of the underlying contradictions between capital and labor, bourgeoisie and proletariat.

In pre-March [1848] Germany, theological considerations were still dominant; it was the relationship of philosophy to religion that gave philosophy its importance. After Hegel's death, the big question among his adherents was: How does philosophy relate to belief and to the church? It was an Hegelian, David Friedrich Strauss, who wrote the earth-shaking *Life of Jesus* (1835). He compared the various schisms in the Hegelian group with the various parties in Parliament, which at that time in France had come to be called the Right, the Center, and the Left. Around 1840 the Hegelian Left indulged, with growing vehemence, in attacks on traditional ways of life and belief. Theologians continued to be in the forefront. Especially outstanding were two men of keen intellect—Ludwig Feuerbach and Bruno Bauer. These became of special importance to Marx. The friendship with Bauer, ten years his senior, began after the eighteen-year-old Marx withdrew from his first year at Bonn and moved to the University of Berlin. There Bauer, an unsalaried lectuer (*Privatdozent*), was fully imbued with Hegelian concepts. Shortly after this (1838), through his father's death, the fiery young Marx lost the guidance he especially needed. At that time he was already engaged to be married to Jenny von Westphalen, a neighbor's daughter. This good German woman, endowed with Rhenish cheerfulness, became the sun of his otherwise troubled life.

On April 15, 1841, Marx graduated in Jena *in absentia* with a Doctor of Philosophy degree. His dissertation was entitled "The Difference Between the Democritean and Epicurean Philosophy of Nature" (*"Über die Differenz zwischen der demokritischen und epikureischen Naturphilosophie"*). The goal of Marx, the Hegelian, was then to become a university lecturer in philosophy. However, a time of unrest and disappointment followed. He did not follow an academic career, and the thorny path ahead of him was sensed even before the thorns had a chance to grow. He must have been deeply impressed by the fact that his friend, Bruno Bauer, who had been admitted as a professor at Bonn University and then was dismissed by decree of the Prussian Ministry because of his book *Critique of the Evangelical History of the Synoptics (Kritik der evangelischen Geschichte der Synoptiker)*, published in three volumes in 1841. Bauer had moved from Berlin to Bonn, where Minister Altenstein had planned to have him receive a professorship. Bauer was anxious to have his young friend, Marx, join him in Bonn in publishing a radical journal. At that time Marx was still considering using his studies in a practical, secure career. He thought of becoming a lawyer, which would enable him to support his wife-to-be and his mother. To be sure, he had not as yet passed any formal law examinations. Bauer declared Marx's practical intentions to be "nonsense" saying, "Theory is now the strongest practice and we cannot yet predict in what great sense it will become practical."

Marx was still living securely within bourgeois society. He wanted to dedicate his dissertation, which he was preparing for publication, to the father of his betrothed, "his faithful fatherly friend, the administrative councilor (Geheime Regierungsrat) Ludwig von Westphalen." It is doubtful that Marx entertained the idea of publishing the journal [with Bauer in

Bonn], which, according to Bauer, was to be even more radical than the *Hallische Jahrbücher,* the organ of the well-known Hegelian, Arnold Ruge. In any case, the project fell through, and in a way Bauer's fate was to become Marx's fate. It is reported that Bauer's lack of success swayed Marx from an academic career. Marx also had to fear being rejected in an academic career, not for his political but for his philosophical position, which was still that of the young Hegelians. He now entered the career of those "people who had missed their calling." He became a journalist. [In 1842 Marx joined the staff of the *Rheinische Zeitung.*] To be sure, he became a journalist of a special type; his true occupation was that of a private scholar and free-lance writer.

The *Rheinische Zeitung,* founded by leading Rhineland citizens, enjoyed the support of the Prussian government because this paper's objective was to counteract the influence of the respected *Koelnische Zeitung,* which at that time was "sailing in ultramontane waters."[2] The new newspaper was intended to become for Prussia and north Germany what the *Augsburger Allgemeine* was for south Germany and Austria, and what in effect the *Koelnische* later did become. If one reads Marx's essays in the *Rheinische,* that is if they can be identified as his, one finds that the philosopher is always present, even when the topic deals with the sessions of the sixth Rhenish Provincial parliament. However, when he writes criticizing an editorial in the *Koelnische*—which had asked whether religious matters should be debated philosophically even in newspaper articles—he is in his own element, discussing the relationship between philosophy and religion. The [*Koelnische*] editorial posed another question: Should politics in a so-called Christian state be treated philosophically in a newspaper? The young Marx treats both questions with superior wit, as a man of liberal and enlightened views, deepened by Hegel's philosophy. In his view the state is "the great organism in which lawful, moral, and political freedom has to find its realization, and in which the individual citizen in obeying the state laws obeys only the natural laws of his own reason, of the reason of humanity."

His bitter critique of the philosophical manifesto of the historical school of law, the Natural Law of "Knight" Hugo, is in the same vein. Marx characterizes him as an absolute skeptic. He notes that just as Kant's philosophy can be seen as the German theory of the French Revolution, so Hugo's Natural Law can be seen as the German theory of the *ancien régime*. Marx characterizes it as sloppy triviality which, he says, is also found behind the exaggerated pathos common to all the later proponents of the historical school of law. As a progressive liberal, Marx furthermore guards himself against the reproach made by the *Augsburger Allgemeine* that the *Rheinische Zeitung* is flirting with "communism." Marx wrote that the *Rheinische Zeitung* did not even attribute any theoretical reality to the communist ideas "in their present form," much less could the newspaper wish for or consider possible their political realization. But the newspaper (i.e., Marx) wanted to study these ideas critically as they are contained in writings by Leroux, Considérant, and especially Proudhon. [Here he means the latter's sagacious work, *Qu'est-ce que la Propriété? (What Is Property?)*.]

According to Marx, there is no danger in practical efforts or experiments, but the theoretical exposition of these ideas is the real danger; "for, practical experiments, even mass experiments, if they tend to become dangerous can be answered by means of cannons. However, ideas which have mastered our intellect, which have conquered our minds, which have been tied to our conscience by our intelligence, are chains from which one cannot tear oneself without tearing one's heart; these are demons which can only be vanquished by surrender." These were mighty words, full of presentiments, from which it can be deduced that young Marx was already challenged by these ideas, that they were touching him gingerly as a foreboding of his future fate. Many years later he saw in these remarks only a "confession" that his studies up to that time had not allowed him to judge the direction in which the French developments were leading, but that he had to solve the doubts which beset him. In this polemic he speaks of a "fear of conscience engendered by the rebellion of a man's subjective wishes against the objective insights of his own intelligence."

Obviously, he was deeply impressed by what he read about communism as "a highly serious topic of the day for France and England," and about "problems which two nations are working to master." He had a short notice printed in the *Rheinische Zeitung* about the book by the Schleswig-Holsteiner, Lorenz Stein, *Socialism and Communism in Present-Day France (Sozialismus und Kommunismus des heutigen Frankreichs).* This book was epoch-making among German intellectuals. Sombart, like others, pointed out that this work must have had great importance for Marx and must have left a lasting impression on him. In this book Marx found socialism designated as a science and a philosophical system, but communism was branded as a pure negation of the old order without direct aim and objectives.

The *Rheinische Zeitung* "for Politics, Trade, and Commerce" was short-lived. The government of the "romantic king" [Friedrich Wilhelm IV] had encouraged freedom of the press somewhat, but was soon frightened by the storms that howled through the newspapers. The government of Saxonia was equally alarmed by the writings of Arnold Ruge, whose articles appeared in the *Deutsche Jahrbücher* in Dresden after the *Hallische Jahrbücher* had been banned. However, publication of the *Deutsche Jahrbücher* was also prohibited in Dresden. Subsequently, Ruge, who represented the German radicalism of that period, moved to Paris. [Marx was already in Paris, having moved there after the demise of the *Rheinische Zeitung*.] In France alone, Ruge saw the political principle, the pure principle of human freedom in Europe. In Marx he found a companion-in-exile, and Marx's brilliant talents did not escape the older man. The two collaborated in publishing the *Deutsch-Französischen Jahrbücher,* whose title is reminiscent of Ruge's earlier undertakings. Characteristic of the period prior to March 1848 was the short life of newspapers and journals. Only one double issue of the journal was published. A high official reported that the journal had a marked tendency toward "insurrection of thought as a means to revolution." Even some German refugees thought the journal went too far. The Prussian government labeled the journal's contents as attempted high treason and a crime against the sovereign; two hundred and thirty copies were stopped at the border of the Palatinate; arrest warrants were sworn out for Ruge, Marx, and Heinrich Heine (who had satirized Ludwig von Bayern in the journal) in case they crossed the Prussian border. The yearbook enterprise failed before it could be determined whether or not it could be legally suppressed under French publication laws. The rather rare German publication originating in Paris is especially memorable for Marx's contributions to it. Immediately following Ruge's "plan," which filled the first page of the publication, there is an exchange of letters among Ruge, Marx, and the young Russian, Bakunin. This correspondence is initiated by a letter from Marx to Ruge "On the Canal Boat to D" (probably Dordrecht) written in March 1843. Marx talks about the approaching revolution as the fate of Germany. When Ruge writes from Berlin saying that Marx's belief is merely wishful thinking, that actually this species (the German people) is not born to be free, Marx answers with these good words: "No people will despair, and even if its hope is based on ignorance, it will, after many a year all of a sudden through a judicious move, realize its pious wishes." For the time being, Ruge appeared to be right.

The collaboration of the "Rugianer" [i.e., the followers of Ruge] was sought by a German newspaper that appeared in Paris with some support of the German legation and which professed to "moderate progressiveness." Soon the paper, called *Vorwärts*, was accused of communist tendencies. The Prussian legation asked for the expulsion of the communists; the publisher of *Vorwärts* was jailed because he did not raise the required bail; the liberal-minded bourgeois king [Louis Philippe] wanted to eliminate German revolutionary ideas from Paris. A continuation of *Vorwärts*, which had planned to change to a monthly journal, had become impossible. In January 1845 Minister Guizot decreed Marx's exportation. Marx, who had established his family in Paris, moved first to Liège, and then to Brussels. His years of wandering had begun. He had not come to Paris as a refugee, but once banned from there he remained a refugee for the rest of his life.

While still living in the Rhineland, Marx, like other radicals, was anxious to learn something about foreign social theories.

Even before he enlarged his knowledge through Lorenz Stein, he must have been aware of Proudhon's essay on property. In Paris, he became a friend of Proudhon. He made a great effort to imbue Proudhon with German—that is, Hegelian—philosophy. At the same time he started to free himself from this philosophy. For the journal published by Ruge and himself, he authored a critique of the Hegelian *Philosophy of Right*. Despite his legal training and his political radicalism, religion stood in the foreground of Marx's early thinking. His friend, Bruno Bauer, had been even more radical than Strauss in exposing the documents of the New Testament as "tendentious writings," but religion still maintained its Hegelian meaning as idea, the Christian religion being its highest manifestation. Feuerbach's *Essence of Christendom (Wesen des Christentums)*, published like other important works in 1841, consummated the dissolution of the Hegelian school in this field.

"For Germany, the criticism of religion has been largely completed; and the criticism of religion is the premise of all criticism."[3] With these words Marx opened the introduction to his "Contribution to the Critique of Hegel's Philosophy of Right," about which nothing more than this introduction was ever known. This marked a great change in Marx's thinking. Written in typical school language and showing preference for antithetical statements which so characterized the young philosopher as a journalist, Marx tries to develop a thesis from concepts that "the criticism of heaven [should be] . . . transformed into the criticism of earth, the criticism of religion into the criticism of the law, the criticism of theology into a criticism of politics."[4] He distinguishes a practical and a theoretical political party in Germany. The former would negate philosophy without realizing it; the latter, vice versa. The criticism of German philosophy of right and of the state is, therefore, the critical analysis of the modern state and of the reality connected with it, as well as a decided negation of the hitherto existing German political and legal consciousness, the most distinguished, most scientific expression of which is the speculative philosophy of right itself. This criticism is meant to end in tasks which can be solved in only one way: practical action *"à la hauteur des principes,"* that is, in a revolution which ought to elevate Germany not only to the official level of modern nations, but to the human apex which would be the immediate future for these nations. "It is clear that the arm of criticism cannot replace the criticism of arms. Material force can only be overthrown by material force; (but) even theory becomes a material force when it has seized the masses."[5]

Here Marx's thoughts go back to the criticism of religion that ends with the doctrine that man is the supreme being for man, that is, with the "categorical imperative to overthrow all conditions in which man is an abased, enslaved, abandoned, contemptible being."[6] Even Germany's revolutionary past, the Reformation, had followed this path. However, the "material foundation" of a radical German revolution can be tested in the French model in which one class hissed "at its adversary the defiant phrase: I am nothing and should be everything"[7]; and can find therein a positive possibility for a German emancipation. Marx finds and discusses this emancipation as follows: "A class [*Klasse*] must be formed which has *radical chains* . . . an estate [*Stand*] which is the dissolution of all estates [*Stände*], a sphere of society which has a universal character because its sufferings are universal, and which does not claim a *particular redress* because the wrong which is done to it is not a *particular wrong* but *wrong in general* . . . which cannot emancipate itself without emancipating itself from all the other spheres of society, . . . which is, in short, a *total loss* of humanity and which can only redeem itself by a *total redemption of humanity*. This dissolution of society, as a particular class [*Stand*], is the *proletariat*."[8] After further exposition on the formation of the proletariat in Germany as "the mass resulting from the *disintegration* of society and above all from the disintegration of the middle class" Marx states: "Just as philosophy finds its *material* weapons in the proletariat, so the proletariat finds its *intellectual* weapons in philosophy. And once the lightning of thought has penetrated deeply into this virgin soil of the people, the Germans will emancipate themselves and become men."[9]

In a brief outline of his intellectual development, which he wrote in 1859,[10] Marx indicated that his "critical revision of the Hegelian Philosophy of Right" had been his first attempt to come to terms with various doubts which beset him at that time. He then summarizes the result of these studies in one sentence which culminates in the judgment that the anatomy of bourgeois society is to be sought in the political economy. It appears, therefore, that Marx finished more than the introduction to his critique on Hegel; however, apparently nothing of this exposition was preserved. Only from other fragments of that time are we able to get an idea about the development of his thinking.

The *Pariser Jahrbücher (Paris Yearbooks)* also contained two important articles "on the Jewish question," which referred to two essays by Bruno Bauer, who had been Marx's teacher in philosophy. Therefore, in this case, the confrontation with Hegel at that time meant a confrontation with Bauer. We shall now deal with the first of the two essays. Bauer had asked these questions: What is the nature of the Jew who is to be emancipated? What is the nature of the Christian state which is to emancipate him? Bauer's answer stressed the religious opposition, and emancipation from religion was made a condition for both the Jew and the Christian state. The state which presupposes religion is no true, actual state. Marx objects that Bauer did not also ask himself: What kind of emancipation is involved? In his criticism of the religious and the secular state he concludes: "The political emancipation of the Jew or the Christian or the religious man in general is the emancipation of the state from Judaism, Christianity, and religion in general."[11] Through his further discussion, Marx wanted to bring to life the contrast between "bourgeois" society (Gesellschaft) and the state in the Hegelian sense. The consistent state is the state which leaves religion to society as a purely private matter. "Religion is no longer the spirit of the state. . . , it has become the spirit of civil society, of the sphere of egoism, and of the *bellum omnium contra omnes.*" "It is no longer the essence of community, but the essence of differentiation. . . . The infinite fragmentation of religion in North America, for example, already gives it the external form of a purely private affair. It has been relegated among the numerous private interests and exiled from the life of the community as such."[12] The difference between the so-called Christian state and the democratic state, as the real state, is further stressed. In the democratic state the evolution of the human spirit, whose expression is the religious spirit, manifests and constitutes itself in its secular form. Not Christianity but the human basis of Christianity is the basis of this state.

The question whether the Jew could claim the "human rights" for himself was asked and given a negative answer by Bauer. He explained that the Jew was exempted because of his eternal isolation which gave him his special nature and his true highest being. Contrary to this, Marx wanted to emphasize the fact that the rights of man in distinction to the rights of the citizen, are the rights of a member of bourgeois society, that is, of egoistic man separated from other men and from the community. He elaborates this with reference to the Constitution of 1793 which speaks of the "inalienable" rights of liberty, equality, security, property. "Man is far from being considered . . . as a species-being; on the contrary, species-life itself, i.e., society, appears as a system which is external to the individual and a limitation of his original independence . . ."[13] It is puzzling to Marx that this proclamation was made at a time when the French nation was about to become a political entity which could save itself only through heroic devotion, when egoism becomes a punishable act like a crime. It is puzzling to him that especially at this point in time political life was recognized as a mere means whose goal was the preservation of bourgeois society. (It is true that revolutionary practices had been flagrantly contradicting theory.) "But the problem is simply answered. Political emancipation is at the same time the dissolution of the old society, that is, of feudalism; political revolution is the revolution of civil society. . . . It dissolved civil society into its basic elements: on the one hand, individuals; on the other hand, the material and cultural elements which form the life experiences . . . of these individuals."[14] Thus, the acknowledgement of freedom for the egoistical man becomes the acknowledgement of the unrestrained movements of these elements. This abstraction of political man was rightly described by Rousseau: "Human emancipation will only be complete when the real, individual man absorbs into himself the abstract citizen; when as an individual man in his everyday

life, in his work, and in his relationships, he has become a
species-being; and when he has recognized and organized his
own powers *(forces propres)* as social powers so that he no
longer separates this social power from himself as political
power."[15]

With this deep, thought-provoking statement, the first essay
"On the Jewish Question" closes. We can now see how the
philosopher of law, Marx, begins to separate himself from Hegel through a train of thought which might be described as
sociological, and how he tries to overcome the form of liberalism which had been theoretically radicalized by the Hegelian
Left. The consideration is ethically colored. It is a thorough
criticism of the egoism of civil society and of the freedom of
the egoistical man which is seen as the reason for the dissolution of feudal society through the revolution. This reason, the
freedom of the egoistical man, now became the basis of the
political state. The following sentences are characteristic:
"Thus, man was not liberated from religion, he received religious liberty. He was not liberated from property; he received
the liberty to own property. He was not liberated from the
egoism of business; he received the liberty to engage in business."[16] Brilliant antitheses still pleased the young writer. Furthermore, they mark the peculiar sharpness of his Jewish mentality.

NOTES AND REFERENCES

1. T.N.: See p. 43 on Marx leaving for London in 1849.
2. T.N.: Ultramontane was a political slogan used against the German Catholics, who were said to be taking orders from Rome in *all* areas of life.
3. T.N.: From "Contribution to the Critique of Hegel's Philosophy of Right." (Hereafter abbreviated to CCHPR.) See Thomas Bottomore, *Karl Marx—Early Writings* (London: C. A. Watts & Co., 1963), p. 43.
4. T.N.: Ibid., p. xiii.
5. T.N.: Ibid., p. 52.
6. T.N.: Ibid.
7. T.N.:Ibid., p. 56.
8. T.N.: Ibid., p. 58.
9. T.N.: Ibid., p. 59.
10. T.N.: This date may be a typographical error. The chapter was to end with 1843. Bottomore, op. cit., gives between the autumn of 1843 and January 1844 as the first publication date of CCHPR.
11. T.N.: Ibid., p. 10.
12. T.N.: Ibid., p. 15.
13. T.N.: Ibid., p. 26. Compare with *Gemeinschaft und Gesellschaft.*
14. T.N.: Ibid., pp. 27–28.
15. T.N.: Ibid., p. 31.
16. T.N.: Ibid., p. 29.

Chapter 2

STORM AND STRESS—
UP TO THE MOVE TO LONDON
(1843–1850)

Marx, the actual editor, had included in the *Paris Yearbooks* two works of a young man who had already gained the attention of radicals, as well as of governments, as a very radically minded individual. He became known for his literary daring under the name of Frederick Oswald. In Manchester he continued to use his real name, Friedrich Engels. His contributions to the *Yearbooks* were "Outline of a Critique of the National Economy" and "Conditions in England," which were set off against Carlyle's *Past and Present,* and which included long excerpts from this recently published book. The first essay, the "genius sketch," as Marx referred to it many years later, must have left the stronger impression on Marx's questioning intellect. After its publication, Marx engaged in a constant written exchange of ideas with Engels.

Marx had then barely begun his studies of the works on economics. Based on his insufficient knowledge at that time, he characterized Ricardo as cynical and spoke of McCulloch as one of the best and most well-known national economists.

In his first essay, Engels discusses exchange, competition, monopoly, value, production costs, capital and labor, and the economic crises which in the past eighty years had appeared as regularly as had the great epidemics, "and brought more misery and immorality than the latter." This, wrote Engels, is a law of competition which could only maintain itself through periodic revolutions, a law of nature which rests on the lack of consciousness of the participants; it is no law of the intellect. Engels thought that the production powers available to humanity were immeasurable, that the productivity of the soil through the use of capital, labor, and science could be increased indefinitely. The contradiction between wealth and poverty existing at the same time, the fact "that people starve in the midst of plenty," is a real absurdity which has been present in England for some time. This had led, thought Engels, to Malthus' population theory which apparently explains this absurdity, but is actually an infamous, vile doctrine, a horrible blasphemy against nature and humanity. It is the immorality of the economist driven to its extreme, and is, according to Engels, the economic expression for the religious dogma concerning the contradiction between the intellect and nature and the resulting immorality of both. The contradiction, said Engels, has long been dissolved for religion through the dissolution of religion itself.

Engels hoped to have shown that this contradiction is also null and void in the economic sphere, that it its only necessary to amalgamate the present antagonistic interests where each adult produces more than he can eat and children are like trees which abundantly repay the expenditures made for them. Even if it is assumed that the increase in agricultural productivity does not always rise in proportion to labor, there is, nevertheless, a third element—besides soil and labor—namely, science, the progress of which is infinite and is at least as speedy in development as that of the population. Engels points to the advances in agricultural chemistry by Humphrey, Davy, and Justus Liebig asking, "What is impossible for science?" Furthermore, he discusses the centralization of property, which progresses more quickly in commercial and agricultural crises, as a law immanent in private ownership. Monopoly produces free competition, and the latter again produces monopoly. Competition has become a part of all living conditions. It also reaches over into the moral sphere, in that society "produces a demand for crime"—private property has brought humanity to this deep degradation. Science also, especially technology, has become, under present conditions, the ally of capital and land against labor. This has been shown by the history of technological inventions and their effects in England. Engels concludes his article promising shortly to develop to some extent the theme of the horrible immorality of the factory system, and relentlessly to lay bare the hypocrisy of economists which appears there in its full flowering.

We are not attempting here to ascertain the truth of these

views nor what was new in them. For Marx, most of the article must have appeared as true to him and some views must have been new. The whole view must have surprised him by its boldness and acuteness. At that time in Germany, List had gained a reputation as a resolute adversary of free trade (which was otherwise considered as the last word in the science of "national economics"); until then the German writers on social matters had revealed hardly any knowledge in this area. Engels possessed such knowledge, but it had not increased his respect for capitalistic political economics. His "Outline of a Critique of National Economics" begins with this sentence: "National economics is a natural outgrowth of the expansion of trade, and it replaced the simple unscientific huckster[1] [*Schacher*] with an elaborate system of permissible fraud and a complete science of self-enrichment or profit making." The word huckster [*Schacher*] was a favorite expression of the young merchant [Engels]. As it often happens, his rebellion against society originated in a rebellion against his own family, against his strict father. He used every opportunity to manifest his dislike of the huckster [*Schacher*].

And now it is remarkable that this Jewish-German word reappears in the second essay by Marx entitled "On the Jewish Question," which is an answer to an essay by Bruno Bauer published in the book *21 Bogen aus der Schweiz (21 Pages from Switzerland)*, edited by Georg Herwegh. This essay is only one fourth the length of Marx's first article on the "Jewish Question," but its tone is quite different. Here he wanted to eliminate completely the theological content of the Jewish question. He wanted to focus attention on the real, worldly Jew instead of Bauer's "Sabbath Jew." According to Marx, in the first kind of Jew is embedded the secret of his religion. His worldly cult is that of huckster *(Schacher)*, his worldly god, money. "Very well then! In emancipating itself from huckstering and money, and thus from real and practical Judaism, our age would emancipate itself."[2] ". . . In the final analysis the emancipation of the Jew is the emancipation of mankind from Judaism, . . . because . . . the practical Jewish spirit has become the practical spirit of the Christian nations."[3] (A phrase which could have served as a motto for the famous book by Sombart,

Die Juden und das Wirtschaftsleben.) "As soon as society suc-
ceeds in abolishing the empirical essence of Judaism—huckstering and its preconditions—the Jew becomes impossible,
because . . . the conflict between the individual, sensuous existence of man and his species-existence is abolished."[4] I believe
that this view developed under the immediate impression of
Engels' manuscripts, perhaps also from the letters accompanying and following the manuscripts.

The letter-exchange led Engels to pay Marx a ten-day visit
—perhaps a house-visit—in the late summer of 1844 in Paris.
These were eventful days. The acquaintance grew into a lifelong brotherhood. Both young men had much more in common than a burning interest in socialism and communism and
an indignation about the immorality of the present society and
its order. Both had partaken of the Hegelian philosophy, Engels rather hurriedly and easily, Marx slowly, laboriously, not
neglecting the perilous depths. Both were swept away by the
dissolution of this school as it became manifest in Feuerbach's
thinking. For, until then the problem of religion was well in
the center of their consciousness, as was the case for the Young
Germany and the Hegelian "Left" in general; radicalism only
gropingly dared to enter the field of politics. Because they felt
drawn in this direction and wanted to move from theory to
"practice," the *Essence of Christianity* was for them experienced as liberation. To them, Feuerbach, its author, appeared as the new Socrates who brought philosophy back from
heaven to earth. For them, the events of the seventeenth century, when natural science with its study of matter and motion
dissolved the spiritualism of the peripatetic school and brought
out the "reformed philosophy" in Galilei, Hobbes, Descartes,
Gassendi, were being repeated in a different form. Thus,
materialism and humanism entered a union in the eyes of the
German youth who felt uncomfortable with actionless German idealism. According to Engels (when writing on Carlyle),
not only Feuerbach but also Bruno Bauer "extended the meaning of the word 'theology' to include the total untruth and
hypocrisy of the present day." He said that German philosophy
had solved the question "What is God?" by saying "God is
man." A person had to find the truth in his own heart. This

newest German philosophy became for Engels the free humanistic view which also left behind Carlyle's pantheism.

With this fresh inspiration, Engels came to Marx. He found him well prepared. He (and without doubt Engels) had been greatly agitated by the June revolt of the Silesian weavers. Marx had become aware of the contrast between Arnold Ruge, the leader of radicalism at that time, and himself. In an article in the Parisian *Vorwärts,* Marx had unloaded some of his anger; Ruge, who hid himself behind a nameless "Prussian," had not credited the revolt with any more general significance than some local flood or food shortage. German society had, according to Ruge, not even reached the point of having a presentiment of the coming "reform." Marx points to the pauperism of England, the general significance of which had also escaped the consciousness of the bourgeoisie of the country, of its press, and even of its economics; it is, therefore, no typical trait of the unpolitical German society and of the king of Prussia to seek the means against pauperism in governmental and welfare measures. Even in England pauperism is being "administrated," although only that kind of pauperism which is desperate enough to let itself be caught and locked up. Napoleon, too, had wanted to eliminate begging at one blow. The state, says Marx, is unable to act otherwise. "The state and the establishment of society—when seen from a political viewpoint—are not two different things. The state is the institution of society *(Gesellschaft)."* In this article, Marx furthermore discusses the disparity, baseness, and slavery of bourgeois society as the natural foundation of the modern state. And here we again meet up with the "modern hucksterism" *("moderne Schacherwelt").* Here, as well as in his remarks on the conditions in England, we notice the influence of Engels.

Marx, however, ascribes to the Silesian weaver revolt a more theoretical significance and more conscious character than to any of the French and English worker revolts. In "Weitling's gifted writings" he sees a brilliant testimony for the education and the educability of the German worker. He prophesies for "the German Cinderella" (the German worker) a future in which it will rise to the stature of an athlete, since already in its infancy "the proletariat is wearing giant shoes, while the political shoes of the German bourgeoisie are dwarflike and worn out." Only in socialism can a philosophical nation find its adequate practice; that is, only in the proletariat can the working element find its liberation. The "Prussian" (Ruge) had ended his essay with the sentence: "A social revolution without a political soul (that is, without an organizing comprehension from the viewpoint of the whole) is impossible." Marx declares a social revolution "with" a political soul is a mere paraphrasing of a revolution and senseless. On the other hand, a political revolution with a social soul makes sense. Socialism needs the political action of a revolution, insofar as destruction and dissolution are necessary. "But where its organizing action begins, where its self-interest, its soul comes to the fore, there socialism casts off the political hull."

Marx's divorce from Ruge, the great prophet of political radicalism was thereby consummated. It was not a difficult step for Marx. Each felt superior to the other, but as a socialist, Marx wanted to be on his own to aspire to the socialistic transformation. He had this in common with Engels, who also embodied this striving. However, Engels was more daring and reckless. But Engels found that his view-sharing comrade—as such he looked upon Marx from now on—was just about to engage in an intellectual fight in still another direction. For Engels, both Feuerbach and Bruno Bauer were still considered as the perfection of German philosophy. Marx directed Engels' attention to the polemics contained in the *Allgemeine Literaturzeitung* which was at that time published by Bauer for a short period. Marx wanted to defend himself. He found it necessary to break with Bauer, who was one of his oldest friends and who had been most influential in the development of Marx's liberal Hegelianism. Bauer wanted to stress the absolute critique, and through it, the infinite self-consciousness which is inspired by a feeling of sublimity over the masses. Even more than Bauer himself, great scholar that he was, his colleagues (among them his brother Edgar) appear to have provoked a satirical reply from Marx.

Marx wanted to write the "Criticism of the Critical Critique" *("Kritik der kritischen Kritik")*, wishing Engels to help, who cheerfully agreed. Jokingly, Marx had spoken of the "Holy

Family" (the Bauer family, for a third brother was a publisher). The title pleased Marx's publisher, but it somewhat frightened Engels who had not wished to have his name appear on the title page, because he feared his "old man" might be offended. *The Holy Family (Die heilige Familie)* appeared in 1845. Engels' part was small, but the two names were now united and remained so.

At that time both men found themselves united in "realistic humanism," that is, with Feuerbach, whom Engels enthusiastically admired. This realistic humanism, thus begins the introduction, has a no more dangerous foe in Germany than spiritualism or speculative idealism. "What we are attacking in Bauer's criticism is just that speculation which reproduces itself as caricature." Furthermore, Marx talks about the nonsense of German speculation, about the illusions of speculative philosophy, as if Schopenhauer were talking about Schelling and Hegel. In the chapter on the critical battle against French materialism, Marx says that, insofar as this form of materialism is a direct continuation of English materialism, it is a promising tendency since it would lead directly toward socialism and communism. The scientifically minded French communists Dézamy, Gay, etc., he says, as well as Owen, had developed the doctrine of materialism as a doctrine of "realistic humanism" and as a logical basis of communism. The philosophical position which Marx represents here, however, was to undergo great changes later on. The same holds also for his sociological orientation which in *The Holy Family* is above all based on Proudhon, who in Marx's view had done an excellent piece of work in criticizing—as an economist—national economics by means of unmasking private property as the universal adulterator of economic conditions. At the end of the Preface, the authors announce independent essays in which each one promises to write about their positive views and therefore about their positive relationship to the more recent philosophical and social doctrines.

This plan brought Engels to Brussels in the spring of 1845, where Marx had just moved. In the summer they traveled together to England. Engels saw it as his task to acquaint Marx with English conditions and with the leaders of the still flourishing Chartism. After returning to Brussels, they eagerly worked on the critique of the post-Hegelian philosophy. Marx was never quite as enamoured with Feuerbach as was his young friend. He did acknowledge him, however, in *The Holy Family*. There, Marx states that Feuerbach dissolved the metaphysical absolute spirit into the "real human person on the basis of nature," and that he had thereby brought the criticism of religion to its consummation, and at the same time laid "the great and masterful foundations for the criticism of the Hegelian speculation and thus of all forms of metaphysics." The eleven notations or theses (published in the appendix of the essay on Feuerbach by Engels), written by Marx in the spring of 1845, start out with a listing of the major deficiencies of all heretofore existing kinds of materialism, including that of Feuerbach. Marx states that the phenomenon, the reality, the sensuousness are only grasped in their formal aspects of the object or of perception, but not as a human, mental activity, as practice, i.e., not subjectively. The human being, which for Feuerbach replaces the religious being, is in reality, said Marx, the ensemble of social conditions; the religious sentiment itself is a product of society. The "new" materialism which Marx wanted to initiate, takes the *human* society as its point of reference while the old materialism, including that of Feuerbach, refers to *bourgeois* society.

This accent on "Practice" was wholly in accord with Engels' wishes. Every so often he would speak rather disparagingly about "theory." He was concerned with propaganda because he hoped to agitate his "wild, hot-blooded dyers and bleachers" of the Wuppertal region into action. He was particularly delighted to introduce communistic literature into Germany and intended to start a "library" of translations beginning with Fourier. Moritz Hess, the most decisive socialist of the older generation, was living in Barmen at this time when Engels was corresponding with Marx about these plans (before they met in Brussels). Both looked upon Hess as one of their own, but more as an ideologist, since so far all of socialism appeared to them to be merely an ideology.

In Brussels they decided to work out together the contrast between their view and the ideological view of German philos-

ophy. The work, the title of which accordingly was *Die Deutsche Ideologie (The German Ideology)*, has never been published, but the handwritten manuscript was largely preserved.[5] The first volume, while taking issue with Feuerbach
and Bauer, also disagreed with Max Stirner. Stirner, they said,
wanted to outdo both Feuerbach and Bauer with an absolute
individualism and egoism. The second volume criticizes previous German socialism in order to confront it with the new
"communism" which had been welded together with the new
"historical" materialism.

Already in 1845, four socialist journals were appearing, one
of them, *The Mirror of Society (Gesellschaftspiegel)*, was
founded by Engels in collaboration with Hess, to depict
therein "the social misery and the bourgeois régime." In a
speech in Elberfeld, Hess defined the idea of communism as
"life's law of love applied to social life." This was not according to Engels' taste; but still less were he and Marx pleased
with Karl Grün who, as a disciple of Feuerbach, was proclaim-
ing the "true socialism," and, because he lived in Paris, was
trying to fit Proudhon into the German philosophy, as Marx
had tried to do in like manner before him. A break also occurred between them and Weitling, the Christian communist,
who appeared in Brussels in 1846, and whose followers num-
bered many German journeymen. Until then, Weitling had
been the head of "German" communism, as Cabet had been
the head of the "French." Marx and Engels declared themselves as standing for "communism" and sought thereby to
express that they wanted to belong to the workers' movement
and not stand as intellectuals outside of it. Most of all, though,
they wanted to be the leaders, to make their point of view
heard. They wanted it to become the only valid and dominating idea, in order to lead the revolution of the proletariat
which they hoped would take place in their lifetime according
to their principles.

This intent must explain their next steps. Before he arrived
in Brussels, Engels had already finished his very decisive work
The Condition of theWorking Class in England. He had gone
his own way, which was characterized by "empiricism and
materialism." It was not difficult for him to settle his account

with his former philosophical conscience, for conscience was a light burden for him. This former philosophical conscience, which as Marx stated in 1859 became manifest in their mutual enterprise of writing the *Ideology*, was not as easily overcome by Marx himself. Marx said that Engels had reached the same result "in a different way" and pointed to *The Condition of the Working Class* as evidence. However, in this book, philosophy is hardly mentioned, except that Stirner is discussed here and there. Marx had two things in mind by which he and his new friend wanted to countermand not only German philosophy, but also the whole of socialism, insofar as it was a part of this ideology to date: first, that national economics must be studied as the expression of the class consciousness of the bourgeoisie; and second, that the real social conditions, especially those of the working class, must be studied to develop from these findings an active, fighting, proletarian consciousness. The second task was one that Engels had already laid out for himself. At this time he confidently presumed that a developed proletarian consciousness already existed in England and that a social revolution was imminent, but he admitted as an older man, that his youthful eagerness had led him to this prophesy. Probably Marx only hesitantly shared this illusion. His own aim was directed toward political economics, at first under the great impression that Proudhon had left upon him, but later because he became convinced "that the anatomy of bourgeois society had to be sought in the political economy."

The concept of bourgeois society, as Marx wrote in January 1859, had been taken over from Hegel who subsumed under this concept the whole of material living conditions. We have seen that Marx, after he began his intellectual struggle to overcome his severe doubts, constantly pondered over and studied the concepts of the Hegelian philosophy of right or jurisprudence, especially the relationship between state and society *(Gesellschaft)* in the light of political and social movements, changes, and revolutions: this became his most personal domain for which he was predestined by his own intellectual development. The immediate result he marked in these words: "I was led by my studies to the conclusion that legal relations, as well as forms of state, could neither be understood by themselves nor explained by the so-called general progress of the human mind, but that they are rooted in the material conditions of life. . . ."[6]

This idea can indeed already be noticed in the unpublished manuscript *(The Ideology)*, where it is stated that the "production of material life" is the historically primary act, the state is "bourgeois society in action," or the structure through which individuals of the governing classes enforce their interests. After the two comrades had worked together in Brussels until August 1846, Engels went to Paris to sow some propaganda among the "Straubinger"—as they privately called the German journeymen. He met some opposition among the adherents of Weitling, but even more among those of Grün and Proudhon. At this time Marx felt called upon to write against Proudhon who up to then had been an object of veneration for Marx because he was a theoretician who (like Weitling) came directly out of the proletariat. The new work of the *Ouvrier (Worker)*, which Proudhon entitled *Contradictions économiques* or *Philosophie de la misère (Economic Contradictions or Philosophy of Poverty)*, provoked Marx to state his opposition. It gave him an opportunity to develop his own new point of view, shared by Engels, in contradistinction to that of Proudhon. Proudhon had depicted the communists as without knowledge of national economics, as obstinate and utopian dreamers. Although Marx knew that he was not included in this category, he was already thinking about the foundation of the "new" communism which was definitely to rest on science.

The *Misère de la Philosophie (Poverty of Philosophy)* is the first purely economic essay which Marx, who became renowned in this field, wrote. It contains only two chapters, the first one called "A Scientific Discovery"—meaning Proudhon's theory of constituted value—the other, "The Metaphysics of Political Economics." Marx introduces himself as a docile *(gelehriger)* disciple of Ricardo and maintains that he understood him better than Proudhon; Marx further maintains that the value theory of Ricardo was the scientific explanation of real economic life, and that the value theory of Proudhon was only the utopian interpretation of Ricardo's theory. To be sure, notes Marx, Ricardo's language, in which he equates the cost of living of a man to the cost of production, is cynical, but "the cynicism is in the facts and not in the words which express the facts."[7] According to Marx, Proudhon mixes up two measures: the measure of the labor time necessary for the production of a commodity and the measure of the value of labor; therefore, he sees labor wages as an integrating element of price. And when Proudhon determines the constituted value as the relationship of the proportiateness of products, he draws the conclusion that the labor time necessary for the production of a commodity indicates a just relationship to the needs or demands. Marx contradicts him, saying that at a certain point in the evolution of civilization, production begins to be founded on the antagonism of the classes—"no antagonism, no progress."[8] This antagonism is also the basis for the social condition of the consumers. Cotton, potatoes, and gin are therefore the fundamental pillars of bourgeois society, because they cost least labor and are cheapest.

The "metaphysics" deals with: (1) the method, (2) the division of labor and machinery, (3) competition and monopoly, (4) possessions and the rent from landed property, and finally (5) strikes of workers and labor conditions. Here all points of view that are characteristic of the later Marx are developed or at least indicated. It is clear throughout the whole book that the young man was now in all seriousness studying the "anatomy" of bourgeois society. Besides Adam Smith and Ricardo, he mentions Lauderdale, Sismondi, Storsh, Atkinson, Hopkins, Will. Thomson, Edmonds, Bray, John St. Mill, Sadler, the American Cooper, and among the French, the old, Boisguilbert and Quesnay, and the new, Say and Lemontey. The most remarkable thing is how Marx, the critic, works out the contrast between the *économistes* on the one hand and the *socialistes* and *communistes* on the other. "Just as the economists are the scientific representatives of the bourgeois class, so the socialists and the communists are the theoreticians of the proletarian class. So long as the proletariat is not sufficiently developed . . . [and the fight between them and the bourgeoisie has not started and the productive forces are not sufficiently developed] in the bosom of the bourgeoisie itself to enable us to catch a glimpse of the material conditions necessary for the emancipation of the proletariat and for the formation of a new society, these theoreticians [i. e., the socialists and communists] are merely utopians . . . but in the measure that history moves forward, and with the struggle of the proletariat assumes clearer outlines, they no longer need to seek science in their minds; they have only to take note of what is happening before their eyes and become its mouthpiece. . . . They see in poverty nothing but poverty [while they look for science in their minds and make systems before the struggle starts] without seeing in it the revolutionary, subversive side, which will overthrow the old society. From this moment, science, which is a product of the historical movement, has associated itself consciously with it, has ceased to be doctrinaire and has become revolutionary."[9]

The confrontation becomes especially pronounced in the last part of the "metaphysics," which deals with strikes and worker coalitions. "Economists and socialists are in agreement on one point: the condemnation of coalitions . . . the economists say to workers: Do not enter coalitions."[10] They justify this advice by pointing out the damages of strikes, precipitation of the invasion of machines resulting in loss to the laborer, and finally the general uselessness of revolting against the eternal laws of political economy. But the socialists also say to the workers: "Do not enter coalitions!" They also point to the uselessness and to the costs of organization. But in spite of all money questions "you will continue nonetheless to be the workers, and the masters will still continue to be the masters just as before . . ." The economists want the workers to remain in society as it is constituted and as it has been signed and sealed by them in their manuals.

"The socialists want the workers to leave the old society alone to be better able to enter the new society which they have prepared for them with so much foresight. In spite of both of them, in spite of manuals and utopias, coalitions have not ceased for an instant to go forward and grow with the development and growth of modern industry."[11]

Marx continued: A model development is found in England where "the organization of strikes and *trade unions* went on simultaneously with the political struggles of the workers, who now constitute a large political party under the name of Chartists. . . . Once [the struggle] . . . has reached . . . [a certain] point, association takes on political character. . . . [But] the struggle of class against class is a political struggle . . ."[12] In like manner as the bourgeoisie freed itself and founded bourgeois society, so the proletariat will free itself and establish a new society. In the form of strikes, coalitions, and in other ways the proletarians achieve their organization as a class before our very eyes. "[But] the condition for the emancipation of the working class is the abolition of every class, just as the condition for the liberation of the third estate, . . . was the abolition of all estates . . ."[13] Antagonism will discontinue, and therewith, also political power in its true sense, because the latter is nothing but the expression of antagonism in bourgeois society. Only when the latter ends will "social evolutions . . . cease to be political revolutions."[14]

The paper against Proudhon shows us the thinking and also the theoretical consciousness of Marx, the sociologist, at its height. In no place does he speak here as if he were the representative of a political party. He wanted to stand outside of party politics as a spectator, as a seer, and as such he dares to prophesy the outcome of the class struggle he observes. However, there is an undertone throughout his work from which one can note that he is longing for this future (the emancipation of the working class) and would welcome it with all his heart. Such an undertone is indicative, for, *"der Ton macht die Musik"* (the sound gives the meaning). But nothing gives evidence of an explicit inclination or even endeavor on his part to enlighten the more instinctive, although rightly oriented, labor movement "with the torch light of science." To be sure, Marx was "in the midst" even more so in Brussels than in Paris because he was surrounded by persons with a radical consciousness who were laying plans for an "abolition of private property," the liberation of the proletariat, and other conquests by revolt. Marx followed them only hesitatingly. With Engels, he had founded, in the Belgian capital, a German Workers' Association, which stood completely under his influence, so that people began to talk about a Marx Party. One of the most interesting figures in this union was the "red Wolff," a Silesian farmer's son, called by his friends "Lupus," who until his death in 1864 in Manchester, remained loyal to both leaders. Marx was left the legacy of his small estate. In turn, Marx dedicated the first volume of the *Capital*, published in 1867, to the memory of his unforgettable friend, the heroic, loyal, genuine champion of the proletariat.

There was also an international association of radical thought by the name of *Fraternal Democrats*. It also moved to Brussels, and Marx soon became vice president of the Brussels branch, which had the name "Democratic Society for the Unification of all Countries." In this society, which was public in nature, an international secret organization, called "The League of the Just" *(Bund der Gerechten)* was represented by Schapper, a typesetter, who later became a language teacher (originally he was a German forestry student); by Moll, a watchmaker; and others. Both of these men had helped to transplant this organization from Paris to London. The League of the Just was founded in 1836 as the left wing of the republican Outlaw's League, which had been established two years earlier in Paris by German refugees. Both were secret societies. In Paris alone, the League of the Just had three suballiances, the main group being composed of tailors. The influence of Weitling, who also confessed this "religion," was great here. Without joining the League, Marx and Engels tried to dampen his influence with pamphlets and other demonstrations and to lead the League into other paths. Many years later Engels admitted there was hardly a man among them who had ever read a book about economics, "but that did not count, since 'equality,' 'fraternity,' and 'justice' for the time being helped them over every theoretical hindrance." More than the pamphlets, Engels' book *(The Condition)* seems to have influenced the German journeymen outside Germany—especially in England—and more than all writings, the experiences of the years 1846 and 1847. These events also gave more power to the more radical group among the Chartists.

As one of the contributors to their organ, *The Northern Star*, Engels kept in constant contact with the Chartists and fired their courage. It was important for him and Marx to promote the international cooperation of the workers' movement wherever there was a beginning of such. They expected in this activity to inflame various hearths for their viewpoints and teachings from which the sparks could make the flames rise. They had founded an international correspondence committee and kept up a steady correspondence with Paris and London. The center of the League slowly shifted to London and thereby the League itself became international, although the German language remained the language for all. In 1847 the German Workers' Education Association took the name of the Communist Workers' Education Association. In London it was decided to invite Engels, who was in Paris, and Marx, who was in Brussels, to join the League with reference to the fact that there existed as much conviction about the general accuracy of their viewpoints as about the necessity to free the Alliance from the old conspiratorial forms and traditions. This time, the invitation was accepted. The circle which had gathered in Brussels became a "cell" *(Gemeinde)*. Engels went to Paris to work on the three cells there. The first congress met in London in the summer of 1847, a reorganization was decided upon, the name Communist League was selected. Its goal was to be the "overthrow of the bourgeoisie, government by the proletariat, the abolition of the old bourgeois society resting on class conflicts, and the formation of a new society without classes and without private property." Marx did not attend this congress, but Engels did; and one can say with some certainty that he was influential there, even though the meeting was not without struggles. A journal was born, but only one volume of it appeared. For the first time the now famous call "Proletarians of all countries! Unite!" was heard. It was to displace the nice old motto of the League of the Just: "All people are brothers!" The Fraternal Democrats, however, with whom Marx was more strongly connected than Engels, still held views similar to those expressed in the old motto of the League. Marx had met with them in London on November 29, 1847, and helped to celebrate the anniversary of the Polish revolution; he voiced his conviction that the old society was "lost," and his confidence in the victory of the Chartists— another Poland still waited to be liberated in England.

The Second Congress of the League of Communists followed immediately. It was to approve the new statutes and to discuss a "creed" for which drafts were already existent. The debates lasted ten days. Marx took part in them, although obviously he had not come for this purpose. However, Engels had come from Paris, and the two friends met in Ostende and sailed together from there. A few days earlier Engels had written to Marx: "Think a little about the creed. I think it would be best if we did not give it the form of a catechism but called the thing 'Communist Manifesto.'" He also wrote about his draft which he was going to bring. Marx went to London to greet the Fraternal Democrats with his speech about the Poles. They again expressly emphasized to Marx that their slogan was still: "All people are brothers!" However, Marx also participated in the second Communist Congress which, after a ten-day debate, commissioned the two now acknowledged leaders to work out the final form of the draft of the party program which Marx had presented to the congress. Around Christmas 1847, the draft had taken on its final form and was entitled *Manifesto of the Communist Party.* It was published in London in January 1848 and dispatched to the "cells."

It was a daring thing to call this international association, which consisted of a few clubs of young tradesmen in the capital and was not even represented in Germany, a party in the sense that this word had in the German language. One can get an inkling of the import of this event when thinking of the significance which, three score and ten years later, the German Social Democratic Labor Party was actually able to gain while still under the influence of these two leaders. It is now important to study the various meanings of the word "communist."

We know that in the prerevolutionary period in Germany this word had no especially "terrifying" sound, at least not in circles which were not shunning the light. It was used partly in the same vein as "socialist" by a number of theoreticians and writers who made themselves heard on the left bank of the Rhine and particularly in restless Paris, the "Babel on the Seine." Large circles only learned to discriminate between these two terms through the influence of Lorenz Stein in 1842. Within the smaller circles of the young Hegelians, however,

Moses Hess was the most influential advocate of communism who, independent of Stein and in the same years as well as in earlier times, interpreted communism as a humanistic and ethical order of society. In April 1842 he published in the *Rheinische Zeitung,* which Marx was editing, a French proclamation entitled "Communistic Manifesto"! Mayer, in his work on Frederick Engels,[15] stated that this manifesto contained a "survey on the development of communism in France which was designed to demonstrate to the German public that this was indeed an important historical development having already won numerous adherents among the intellectuals, as well as among the common people on the left side of the Rhine. For this reason, communism should no longer be discarded as a madness—in an attitude of bombastic haughtiness —but it had to be studied and appreciated in its true inner value."

The biographer is obviously right in assuming that around this time and under these influences which continued to be relevant for almost three more years, Engels must have finally decided he was in favor of communism. Marx, however, seems to have made this decision two years later as can be seen from his own and Ruge's *Yearbooks.* And even then this decision was one which determined his thinking much more than his action. For Engels, on the contrary, from the very beginning it had always been a decision determining his action. To be sure, Engels also wanted to be and to remain a "German philosopher"; and as such he presented himself to the Chartists during his first stay in England (1843). He always differentiated between "philosophical" communism, which in his eyes was proclaimed in Germany by Hess, and the communism of the German tradesmen, who as journeymen abroad had already sworn to Weitling's doctrine and had organized their foreign groups into secret leagues.[16] Engels wanted to identify himself with Hess, not with Weitling. However, he did recommend Weitling to the Chartists, and he was quite delighted when in 1843 Bluntschli, in his report to the government in Zurich, made this journeymen's communism known to a large public.

In England Engels soon came into close contact with those socialists who followed Owen's line of thought. Engels' aim

was, on the one hand, to introduce a socialist orientation into
Chartism which, as is well known, only pursued political and
democratic objectives and, on the other hand, to inspire English socialism with the strong will and perseverance of Chartism.[17] He tried to make the English comprehend that on the
continent the progress of social reforms had come about
through the conviction of the people that "the future of mankind belongs to communism." This conviction, he said, had
been achieved by the French through politics, by the Germans
through philosophy, just as the English had achieved it
through practice. At that time he praised Proudhon's work on
property (of the year 1838) as the most important and most
philosophical work in French which favored "communism,"
and in accordance with this, Engels' "communism" is also
somewhat anarchical (the "whole trash of the state" is not
"made to last forever" and must disappear again[18]). Under the
influence of Hess, he presented communism as "the legitimate
heir to German philosophy. "Therefore, the Germans would
either have to disavow their great thinkers or confess to communism. With Hess he was particularly counting on the intellectuals. Hess had said at that time, and with good reason, that
the communist agitation of the German journeymen did not
meet with much understanding among the German proletariat.[19]

Of course, this condition did not satisfy Engels, who was a
revolutionary by temperament as well as by his intellectual orientation. He wanted to enlighten the proletariat, he
wanted to teach it, to make it conscious, and he built upon the
cruder, instinctive communist mentality which he had already
noticed in many places. So, he said, in one of his (rather small)
contributions to *The Holy Family*, that "the watered-down
doctrine of Fourier" as preached by the *"Démocratie pacifique,"* is nothing but the social theory of the philanthropical
part of the bourgeoisie: "The common people (Volk) are communists; they are divided into a great number of factions
which are only beginning to form a movement and to overcome their various social differences." This movement, he says,
will culminate in a "wholly practical practice." Furthermore,
he states that the criticism of the French and the English is also

of a practical nature and that their communism is a socialism in which they offer practical, workable rules, in which they not only think but much rather act. Thus, their communism is a living and real criticism of the existing society.

Engels himself did not really know at that time what he understood by the word communism. Already in the beginning of 1843 this word had become a well-known catchword in Germany, as is testified by Bruno Bauer.[20] In his first publicly known letter to Marx (written at the end of September 1844), Engels mentioned his future brother-in-law, Emil Blank, a merchant, and called him the communist from London. He stated that a great propaganda campaign had been carried out in Cologne, that there was in Elberfeld a more or less heterogeneous clique (of communists), that in Barmen, Engels' home town, the president of the police had turned out to be a communist, that a high school teacher, a former school friend of his, had been very much infected. "One may turn wherever one wants, everywhere one stumbles over communists." He said that there was a communist tavern, that Baedeker was a communist bookseller, hence, that intellectuals were participating in great numbers, but . . . "the Germans on the whole are as yet very unclear about the practicability of communism. In order to put an end to this rubbishy situation, I must write a small brochure telling that the whole thing has already been achieved. I shall describe in simple words the practice of communism as it already exists in England and America; this is going to cost me about three days or so, and must be quite enlightening for the guys." But at the same time he wished to act directly upon the common people *(Volk)*. He wrote that if this were possible, "we would soon be on the top, but this is practically impossible, particularly since we writers must keep quiet in order not be caught." He does not say how many days he would have needed for that, but he would certainly not have spent more than three times three days. In his second letter (of November 19, 1844), he reports his agitation in Cologne and Bonn and then about his work on the English proletarians, about his studies of Stirner, Feuerbach, and Hess. At the end of the letter he says that "socialism" is progressing in all parts of Germany except in Berlin. "Those superclever

Berliners will manage to establish a *démocratic pacifique* on the 'Hasenheide' [a wooded area in Berlin] at a time when in the whole of Germany private property is abolished—those guys will certainly never achieve anything more." Our young writer undoubtedly believed that the paradise of this abolition of private property was imminent. Also in the following letters of 1845 Engels gave expression to this youthful enthusiasm for communism which, however, he does differentiate from the subjects with which the other "socialist writers" are dealing.

In the meantime, he had finished *The Condition of the Working Class in England;* the (English) foreword was written in Barmen under the date of March 15, 1845. In this book the chapter on the workers' movements mainly deals with the Chartists, who are depicted as the first true proletarians, then with the socialists, who originally belonged to the bourgeoisie and were, therefore, unable to amalgamate with the working class. "The amalgamation of socialism with Chartism, the reproduction of French communism in England will be the next step and has already been partly initiated." He states that the leaders of the Chartists are almost exclusively socialists; in another place he writes that most Chartist leaders "already now" are Communists. And then, on the last page, one finds the remarkable statement: "And since communism is standing above the antagonism between the proletariat and the bourgeoisie, the better part of the bourgeoisie—which, however, is terribly small and can only count on future recruitments from among the young generation—will find it easier to align with communism than with Chartism, which is exclusively a proletarian movement." In a later essay Engels proclaimed: "Democracy is nowadays communism." With increasing vehemence, he attacks the "German theory" of socialism and its ties to Stein, while "the only German who has really done something, namely Weitling," is either mentioned disparagingly or not at all.

This proselytizing zeal he then carried among the "Straubinger" in Paris in August 1846. Here he had to fight on two fronts, one against the adherents of Weitling, and the other against those of Proudhon and Grün. When they wanted to know what he actually understood by communism, he answered: the objectives of communism are: (1) to enforce the interests of the proletariat in opposition to those of the bourgeoisie; (2) to achieve this through the liquidation of private property and its replacement by common ownership; (3) not to acknowledge any other means than the violent democratic revolution for carrying out these intentions. One year later (in October 1847) Engels engaged in a vehement polemic against Karl Heinzen, the republican and an adherent of Ruge. Here he maintained that communism is not a doctrine but a movement, that it does not start from principles but from facts, that it is the product of large-scale industry, etc. But as far as communism is theoretical, it is, to him, the theoretical expression of the position of the proletariat in the class struggle between the proletariat and the bourgeoisie and thus, the theoretical summary of the conditions necessary for the liberation of the proletariat.[21] In the *"Grundzüge des Kommunismus"* ("Basic Traits of Communism"), which he wrote a few weeks later in the form of a "catechism," Engels answers the first question, "What is communism?" by simply stating that it is "the theory of the conditions necessary for the liberation of the proletariat"—so it has turned out to be theory after all.

How did Marx react to these views and utterances of his friend? We know that since September 1844 their minds, shall we say their souls, had been communicating reciprocally in a most intensive manner. We know that Marx had completely elaborated the "basic line of thought of the *Manifesto*": namely, the idea that economic production and, as a necessary result of it, the social stratification of any historical epoch are always forming the basis for the political and intellectual history of the respective epoch. He had already drawn the conclusions from this idea when Engels came to Brussels in the spring of 1845. We may conclude from this fact and from other hints that the first part of the *Manifesto*, "Bourgeois and Proletarians," had been written by Marx. This section mainly deals with the class struggles, comparing the class struggle between bourgeoisie and proletariat to that which the bourgeoisie fought against feudalism and feudal absolutism; he therefore also discusses the process of organization of the proletarians into a class. This section does not even mention socialism or communism. Even a person who expected from the decline of the bourgeoisie and from the victory of the proletariat merely the destruction of both and the death of European culture, might be willing to approve of this section.

In the second part, "Proletarians and Communists," one finds the statement that the abolition of the so-far existing property relations is not a specifically characteristic trait of communism; what characterizes communism is not the abolition of property per se, but the abolition of bourgeois property. This clearly indicates a correction that Marx inserted in the draft presented by Engels, who had written: "Private property will also have to be abolished. . . . The abolition of private property is even the shortest and most characteristic summary of the transformation of the total social order arising necessarily out of the development of industry. It is therefore rightly emphasized by communists as their principal demand." After characterizing "modern bourgeois private property" as the last and most perfect expression of the manufacture and acquisition of products based on the antagonism of the classes, and on the exploitation of one class by the other, the *Manifesto* continues as follows: "In this sense, communists may reduce their theory to one phrase: abolition of private property." Marx's corrections are even more noticeable here.

Let us now compare the part for which we are sure that Marx was the only author, which he wrote in the two years preceding the *Manifesto*, to the already mentioned *Misère (Poverty of Philosophy)*. Here we encounter his lectures on wage labor and capital given to "laborers" in 1847. Here mentioned, incidentally, is the theorem about the change in the social conditions of production, caused by a change and development in the material means of production (which he elaborated on later, especially in the Preface of 1859). But primarily these lectures contain a sketchy outline of the whole theory of capital as the bourgeois condition of production, for bourgeois society. This theory later forms the subject of his great major work. The exposition is strictly factual, theoretical, dry. The principal statement is that the interests of capital and the interests of wage labor are diametrically opposed to each other. Here and there he depicts the present and future situation of the working class in dim colors: the division of labor and the expansion of machinery increase competition between the workers, so that their wages are shrinking. The labor force is growing in numbers due to the ruin of small entrepreneurs and small rent collectors, who lift up their arms beside those of the workers: "so, the forest of stretched-out arms demanding employment is continuously becoming thicker while the arms themselves are becoming thinner and thinner." The essay, first printed in 1849, closes with a chapter about these crises. Again there is no mention made of socialism and communism. Engels' sounds and thoughts on this are missing. They are also missing in Marx's speech *sur le libre échange* (on free exchange), given in January 1848 at the Democratic Association in Brussels, although it culminated in the statement that "the system of free trade speeds up the social revolution" and that, in this revolutionary sense, he would also vote for free trade.

More characteristic, however, was the manner in which Marx intervened in the dispute between Engels and Heinzen after Engels had declared that to the "avalanche of dirt" which Heinzen had poured over him, he could answer "at the most with a slap in the face," or else not at all. This was in the middle of November 1847. So Marx was supposed to and also wanted to help his friend out of the deadlock. This happened immediately after the appearance of the *Manifesto*. Heinzen had maintained that power is also the representative of property, that all social questions would disappear in the face of the question: monarchy or republic? If communism, as Engels had said, is a movement toward a goal, then this movement would naturally come to a standstill once this goal was achieved or else it would have to transform itself into a new movement.

Marx, who met rudeness by rudeness, maintained by the way that the political dominance of the bourgeois class originated from these modern conditions of production which bourgeois economists declare to be necessary and eternal laws. "If, therefore, the proletariat overthrows the political dominance of the bourgeoisie, then the victory will only be of a temporary nature. It will only be an element serving the bourgeois revolution itself, as in 1794, so long as in the course of

history, in its ongoing 'movement,' the material conditions
have not yet been created which would necessitate the abolition of the bourgeois mode of production, thus also necessi-
tating the definite fall of the political dominance of the bourgeoisie. . . . Men are building a new world . . . from the historical achievements of their declining world. In the course of the
development, they must themselves first produce the material
conditions of a new society, no moral or intentional effort can
free them from this fate. . . . The question of property varies
depending on the varying stage of industrial development in
general, and on the specific stage of industrial development in
the various countries." All these statements put a damper on
the impetuous revolutionary ideas of Engels which he so vio-
lently expressed in his writings of the same period.

Especially in the years between 1845 and 1847, Engels' development had more and more tended in this direction, in
that he not only waited for, but desired and demanded, the
forcible proletarian revolution—first of all in England—and
consequently, also the "abolition" of property together with
the introduction of communism. Despite his greater prudence, Marx was pulled in this direction by the flaming temperament of his friend, but he retained his original identity.
For it was Marx's intellect which became manifest in the pamphlets in which, according to his own words, he had under-
taken a "merciless critique" of the secret doctrines of the
League of the Just, maintaining that the only viable theoretical
basis would be scientific insight into the economic structure of
bourgeois society. It was Marx, who in a popular manner, explained that their objective was not the realization of some
utopian system, but the "self-conscious participation in a historical process of social revolution taking place before our
eyes." This expression also found entry in the *Manifesto* where
it reads: "The theoretical conclusions of the communists . . .
merely express, in general terms, actual relations springing
from an existing class struggle, from a historical movement
going on under our very eyes."[22]

Marx later admitted that the "sectarian movement" had a
right of existence at a time when the proletariat was not yet
sufficiently developed to be able to act as a class, but personally

he never favored sects. For this reason he probably did not sympathize with the League of the Just, and only reluctantly did he continue his work on the "creed" which they had asked him to formulate. Engels had to urge him on, and as late as January 24, 1848, the "Central Office" in London addressed a very energetic reminder to the office in of the Brussels "cell," stating that "the citizen Marx should be informed that further disciplinary punishment would be inflicted on him if the *Manifesto* of the Communist Party, the formulation of which he had assumed responsibility, had not arrived in London by February 1."[23] We do not know whether Marx smiled or became angry at these officials. He had not attended the first congress of the reformed League, and he had attended the second congress more by chance, since he had traveled to London to meet with the Fraternal Democrats. During their joint trip, Engels must have enthusiastically urged Marx to attend. Marx participated in the debates and accepted the mandate to write the *Manifesto* in collaboration with Engels. Despite the fact that he entered the obligation under pressure, Marx was the one who gave the *Manifesto* its shape, although Engels' driving power is noticeable throughout.

Immediately after this unassuming little booklet had been printed, the February Revolution occurred, not at all anticipated by the authors. The provisional government of Paris invited the citizen Marx, who had just been expelled from Brussels by the bourgeois King Leopold, to settle again in Paris. The "Central Office" of the Communist Union had at the same time entrusted the "office of the Brussels cell," i.e., Marx himself, with the leadership, and Marx preferred to resume this duty while living in Paris. In Paris, Marx was kept very occupied opposing the "revolutionary play" of his German communist comrades. He sharply attacked the fantastic idea of Georg Herwegh (called "the lively one") to invade Germany with armed groups.[24] It is also quite interesting to note how Marx, immediately after the March 1848 Revolution in Germany, formulated the "Demands of the Communist Party in Germany." The small program was undoubtedly written by him. Karl Marx's name heads the group of six names forming the "Committee." In the preface to *Enthüllungen über den Kommunistenprozess (Revelations About the Law-suit Against Communists)* of 1885, Engels intended to re-produce this "document," but strangely enough, points 2, 5, 6, 10, 12, and 13 are missing. Of those which he did reproduce, points 1, 3, and 4 are of a political nature (a united, indivisible republic, remuneration of the representatives of the people, general arming of the people); points 7, 8, and 9 deal with agrarian questions (princely and other feudal landed estates, mines and pits were to become state property; agriculture was to be carried on with the most modern scientific means on a large scale on large farms; mortgages were to become state property and payments for rents were to be paid to the state in the form of taxes). Point 11 demands that the state take over all means of transportation; points 14 and 15 demand the cur-tailment of the right of inheritance and the introduction of strong progressive taxation. Point 16 deals with the establish-ment of national workshops, and 17 with the general and free education of the people. The rather moderate character of these demands may surprise many socialists today. Marx was not deceived about the social conditions in Germany; there-fore, he said: "The German proletariat, the middle class people and the peasants *(kleiner Bürger und Bauernstand)* must in their own interest and with all energy work for the realization of the measures listed."

Marx soon returned to Germany. He thought the time had come to re-edit his newspaper, the *Rheinische Zeitung,* in a new form. Starting with June 1, the *Neue Rheinische Zeitung* appeared as an "Organ of Democracy." It sharply criticized the national conventions of Frankfurt and Berlin, the ministry of Camphausen-Hansemann, demanded the revolutionary war against Russia, passionately took sides with the Poles, but called the general fraternization of all peoples a "most trivial form of political twaddle." This paper also enthusiastically de-fended the war against Denmark as a "national war" and criti-cized the truce of Malmoe. But the counterrevolution quickly took its course. Marx had to make personal sacrifices for his newspaper. At times it was suppressed. Ferdinand Freiligrath became a member of the editorial staff. The fight for a refusal to pay taxes and for armed resistance led in February 1849 to a suit before the assizes in Cologne, but after a scholarly and mighty speech given by Marx, the accused were acquitted. The victory of the counterrevolution, however, became more and more obvious. Marx's newspaper, which at first pursued the objective of representing the mutual interests of the bourgeoisie and the proletariat, more and more revealed its revolutionary character; the victory of the labor class was more and more conceived as the only means to overcome feudalism and absolutism. The conflict soon became evident. Marx was banished, and the last issue of the newspaper appeared on May 19, printed on red paper, with a poem on the front page by Freiligrath, which later became famous.

Marx and Engels went to south Germany; they still had hopes for the movement in Baden and in the Palatinate. The Democratic Central Committee, which in the Palatinate was at the helm of the affairs, commissioned Marx to represent the revolutionary party in Paris. So he returned to Paris, while Engels joined the fighters. Marx also moved his family to Paris. They had barely arrived when a police officer appeared at their apartment and politely ordered Karl Marx "et sa dame" to leave Paris within twenty-four hours. They could have chosen to take domicile in Vannes (Morbihan), but Marx had already decided to go to London; and his family followed him. Soon afterward Engels also returned to the great metropolis.

At the same time that the European revolution was dying, the storm and stress period of the two sons of Germany ended. They were indeed sons of Germany, but the literary storm and stress movement had already reached its climax in the decade following the French July Revolution. Yet these two epigones were actors in the movement. Why was this so? They were the last young generation of a more and more consolidating national bourgeoisie seeking new political conditions and political influence. They were the last young generation with vague ideas and manifold strivings, fond of poetry, capable of sacrifices and willing to fight, ready to run full speed at everything, full of boundless wishes and hopes for the nation, for all classes within the nation, especially for the suppressed and suffering classes, for mankind and for humanity. However, combined with all this was a complete lack of political experiences and alas! of political intelligence. Karl Marx and Friedrich Engels, both coming from the Rhineland, the one from a Jewish, the other from a genuine Brandenburg, family, also belonged to this young generation. But they were its most prominent representatives. Their figures grew in the next generations, instead of being swallowed up by them. Their statures grew because they had recognized more clearly and more exactly the true character of the epoch to which they belonged and to which they had adjusted and because they had looked into a far future and realized that all constitutional and legal questions would fade away in front of the social question. They became greater in stature because they foresaw that within the great nations and thus all over the civilized world, the growing contrast between capital and labor would enforce great decisions, on which depended the fate of human culture, a culture which in the course of the last centuries, had made such a rich, brilliant, and splendid development.

They had "recognized something of this," and for this they had to suffer and to atone. Their souls and names were crucified and burned, as far as this was possible, and even today they are still for many people an object of horror and indignation. But those for whom they have become the heralds and prophets of an august future number in the millions in many countries, however much or little real understanding or even congeniality they may have for the two great men. They have succeeded and they live—not even their enemies can deny this triumph of intellect. Although much error and illusion were involved, although the ultimate condition of all things might prove to be quite different from what both had envisaged—they live on—the one more as a thinker and augur, the other as an enthusiast and fighter; the one as a seer, the other as a dreamer, both confidently inspired by great premonitions.

But the end of the revolution also meant, for the time being, the end of their hopes. This was a heavy blow, especially for the sanguine Engels who had been absolutely convinced of the outbreak of the "social" revolution in England. In 1844–45 he had written that the open and direct war of the poor against the rich had now become quite inevitable; he did not believe that the people would put up with another crisis. England is facing "the dawn of a social revolution" he had preached to his educated fellow communists in Elberfeld. The *Manifesto* also considered the Chartists in England and the agrarian reformers in North America as already constituted workers' parties. The relationship between communism and these parties was for Engels self-evident, since communists always aimed at being the most decisive, most progressive part of the workers' parties in all countries.

Those already constituted workers' parties—where did they go? In the beginning of 1848, the year of the revolution, Chartism had already vanished like chaff in the wind. The American national reforms left still fewer traces. And in France? Engels believed that in France the bourgeoisie had already at that time been the ruling power, consequently the proletariat should be able to take over all the more rapidly. But what did happen? Marx and Engels lived through the Second Empire which, at least in the beginning, did not represent a genuine rule of the bourgeoisie. But they also lived to see the rise of the Third Republic, which was a bourgeois régime. In between, there had, of course, been the battle of June 1848, then the insurrection of the Commune in 1871—bloody defeats of the proletariat. We ourselves have been witnesses of its slow political recovery, which ultimately again completely stagnated in consequence of the first World War.

And Germany? In the *Manifesto* one finds the statement: "The communists turn their attention chiefly to Germany, because that country is on the eve of a bourgeois revolution that is bound to be carried out under more advanced conditions of European civilization, and with a much more developed proletariat than that of England in the seventeenth, and of France in the eighteenth, century, and because the bourgeois revolution in Germany will be but the prelude to an immediately following proletarian revolution."[25] World history took its own course and mocked the prophets.

NOTES AND REFERENCES

1. T.N.: In this, as in the previous chapter, we have followed Bottomore, op cit., and translated the word *Schacher* to the English as huckster.
2. T.N.: Karl Marx, "On the Jewish Question," p. 34. Bottomore version, *Karl Marx's Early Writings,* translated and edited by T. Bottomore, (London: C.A. Watts & Co., 1963).
3. T.N.: Ibid.
4. T.N.: Ibid., p. 40.
5. T.N.: Written jointly by Marx and Engels in 1845 and 1846, it was first published in German in 1932. See Karl Marx and Friedrich Engels, *The German Ideology* (Moscow: Progress Publishers, 1964).
6. T.N.: From *A Contribution to the Critique of Political Economy* (Chicago: Charles H. Kerr, 1954), p. 11. First published in 1859.
7. T.N.: From *The Poverty of Philosophy—Answer to the Philosophy of Poverty by M. Proudhon* (Moscow: Foreign Languages Publishing House, Brusssels Foreword by Marx, dated 1847, but no publication date on the volume translated from the French edition of 1847), p. 48. Hereafter designated as P of P.
8. T.N.: Ibid., p. 59.
9. T.N.: Ibid., p. 120.
10. T.N.: Ibid., p. 164.
11. T.N.: Ibid., p. 165.
12. T.N.: Ibid., pp. 165–66.
13. T.N.: Ibid., p. 167.
14. T.N.: Ibid., p. 168.
15. Gustav Mayer, *F. E. in seiner Frühzeit, 1820–1851* (Berlin: Julius Springer, 1920), Vol. I, p. 114.
16. Ibid., p. 120.
17. Ibid., p. 145.
18. Ibid., pp. 150–51.
19. Ibid., p. 153.
20. Ibid., p. 155.
21. Ibid., p. 279.
22. T.N.: S W I 46.
23. Mehring 147.
24. Ibid., p. 160.
25. T.N.: S W I 65.

Chapter 3

UP TO THE CONCLUSION OF THE FIRST
VOLUME OF CAPITAL . . .
(1850–1867)

In the fall of 1849 Marx and Engels were together in London. Marx's first thought was to revive his newspaper in order to prepare effectively for the proletarian world revolution, an event still expected by both. Together with a publisher in Hamburg, they issued, on a commission basis, the monthly journal *Neue Rheinische Zeitung (New Rhenish Newspaper—A Political Economic Review)*. It was, indeed, a strange title for a periodical written in London. No more than four issues appeared; the last one in April 1850. Herein, Engels had described the German Constitutional Campaign *(Reichsverfassungskampagne)* and the German Peasants' War, in accordance with the "materialistic conception of history." Contemporary French history was most important to Marx, and he wanted to clarify for himself its causes and its course. He had come to the conclusion "that the world trade crisis of 1847 had been the actual mother of the February and March Revolutions and, that the newly blossoming industrial prosperity since the middle of 1848 and 1850, had been the invigorating power of the new strong European reaction" (so Engels wrote in 1895). "A new revolution is only possible in the wake of a new crisis. But the latter is just as certain as the former," Engels wrote in the fall of 1850, echoing his friend's sentiments.

In his first essay on the class struggles in France, which includes the events up to June 1848, Marx tries to prove that revolutionary progress had not advanced through its immediate "tragic-comic" achievements, "but inversely, only through creating a compact and mighty counterrevolution, through creating an adversary who needed to be fought, did the opposition party mature into a real revolutionary party."[1]

The exposition rests upon the insight that it was not the whole French bourgeoisie which ruled under Louis Philippe, but only the aristocracy of finance which was a fraction of the old aristocracy having its "high church" in the bank. The February Revolution had to complete the government of the bourgeoisie in that it allowed, besides the finance aristocracy, all other propertied classes into the circle of political power. "The nominal proprietors, who form the great majority of the French people, the *peasants,* through universal suffrage were put in the position of arbiters of the fate of France."[1a] Thus, Marx here says that the large majority is the peasants and not the proletariat which he had so often before proclaimed to constitute the large majority in all developed countries! To be sure, as it is still the case today, everyone was using this expression according to his whims, in that the proletariat was sometimes considered exclusively the class of industrial workers, at other times, it included the latter as well as small bourgeois farm laborers and even all other farmers. Marx continues that the republic, proclaimed by the National Convention as the only legitimate republic, had been a bourgeois republic which, under the pressure of the proletariat, however, had to announce itself as a republic "with social institutions" because "the Parisian proletariat" (the facts demanded that the concept was even further narrowed) was not yet able to transcend the bourgeois republic other than in its ideas or imagination. Actually, he observes that everywhere when the proletariat really came into action, it acted in the service of the bourgeois republic. But it was not enough for the republic to break at once with the social illusions of the February Revolution. Only the defeat in June of the Parisian proletariat, which had been driven to insurrection by the bourgeoisie, was "the real birthplace of the bourgeois republic." But this was also seen by Marx as the precondition for France's seizing the initiative of a European revolution: "The new French revolution is forced to leave its national soil forthwith and *conquer the European terrain,* on which alone the social revolution of the nineteenth century can be accomplished."[2] [Tönnies comments: And yet the nineteenth century has been over for twenty years!]

The second part of the essay describes the direct consequences of the defeat: mass bankruptcy of the small bourgeoisie, increase of the state deficit, triumph of the national guard, conditions of occupation, the change from the right to work into the right to receive alms. Although the right to work is only "a miserable pious wish, . . . behind the right to work stands the power over capital; behind the power over capital, the appropriation of the means of production, their subjection to the associated working class and, therefore, the abolition of wage labor, of capital and of their mutual relations."[3] In France the right to work was not even yet revived (1920). Furthermore, December 10 (the election of the president) is described by Marx as the day of the peasants' insurrection, although the lower rank bourgeoisie and the proletariat also voted *en bloc* for Napoleon. Also described are the Cabinet Barrot, the reinstatement of the salt tax, the proposal of Rateau to dissolve the National Convention, the "assault through petitions" aiming at the same, the Convention's own decision, the suppression of the clubs, the foreign politics of the Republic, the decline of the "miserable convention" and its disappearance, and the election of the "Legislative Convention" with which the Constitutional Republic was established on May 29, 1849. This part concludes with a characterization of the parties which are considered as being socially determined.

The third part deals with the time from June 13, 1849, to March 10, 1850. The first date brought the peaceful demonstration of the democratic small bourgeoisie of Paris and their defeat. The victory of the "party of order" was followed by the adjournment of the Convention in August. When the Convention met again in October, its character was changed—the break with the president was in the air. The latter formed a cabinet of his rank and file and aligned the executive against the legislative body; he united with the aristocracy of finance, which entered the cabinet in the person of a Jew, Fould. The reintroduction of the wine tax brought the peasants into action; the "Social Democracy" party of the Red Republic, now came to the fore as a coalition against the bourgeois dictatorship. "The proletariat did not allow itself to be provoked to *revolt*, because it was on the point of making *revolution.*"[4] The by-elections of March 10, 1850, a victory for the socialists, meant the disavowal of June 1848 , as well as of December 10, and of June 13, 1849. This date bears the motto *Après moi le déluge!* The fourth part of the essay describes the abolition of the general voting right on May 31, 1850. Prefacing it is an exposition of the general prosperity as the moving cause of the reaction.

Through these essays, the abilities of their author come to light: to engage in absorbing, lively narration, to give sharp, satirical characterization, to treat with agility the universal history of the masses and the unfolding of obscure connections, but these qualities reveal themselves as still greater and more powerful in the continuation of these essays which appeared in 1852 as a special publication entitled, *The Eighteenth Brumaire of Louis Napoleon Bonaparte.* To be sure, the continuation had to deny the prognosis which was the culmination of the earlier exposition. The latter awaited a new proletarian revolution with the outbreak of the industrial crisis, which seemed to be in the air in the fall of 1851 after unheard-of prosperity. The prognosis was a mistake. Louis Napoleon was victorious—and now Marx had to explain this victory. *The Eighteenth Brumaire* depicts the pretender at first as the chief of the Parisian "Lumpenproletariat." This type of people, which cannot be recognized as a class, but only as excrement, rubbish, and scum of all classes as a quite indistinct, dissolved mass which is thrown hither and thither (and which the French call *la Bohème),* is depicted in a few colorful lively sketches: deranged rogues with shady means of subsistence, the scissor sharpeners, tinkers, and beggars.

This history at first includes a revised recapitulation of the events which preceded the coup d'état. No mention is made of the wine tax or of the peasants' indignation to it. Obviously, Marx had hoped that the peasants would put themselves under protection of the proletariat. The exposition becomes bitter. "And it took that peculiar malady which since 1848 has raged all over the Continent, *parliamentary cretinism,* which holds those infested by it grip in an imaginary world and robs them of all sense, all memory, all understanding of the rude external world—it took this parliamentary cretinism, for those who had destroyed all conditions of parliamentary power with their

own hands and who were bound to destroy them in their
struggle with the other classes, still to regard their parliamentary victories as victories and to believe they hit the President
by striking at his ministers."[4a] The question of the revision of
the constitution was placed in the forefront and confused the
parties. Crisis and business panic also occurred: "Think of all
this and you will comprehend why in this unspeakable, deafen-
ing chaos of fusion, revision, prorogation, constitution, conspiracy, coalition, emigration, usurpation and revolution, the
bourgeois madly snorts at his parliamentary republic: *Rather
an end with terror than terror without end.*' Bonaparte understood this cry."[5] The coup d'état unmistakenly announced its
coming a long time before it actually occurred: "On the thresh-
old of the February Revolution, the *social republic* appeared
as a phrase, as a prophecy. In the June days of 1848, it was
drowned in the blood of the *Paris proletariat,* but it haunts the
subsequent acts of the drama like a ghost. . . .The French
bourgeoisie balked at the domination of the working proletariat; it has brought the *Lumpenproletariat* to domination . . . for
its head [it had] an adventurer blown in from abroad, raised
on the shield of a drunken soldiery, which he has bought with
liquor and sausages, and which he must continually ply with
sausage anew. . . . And yet, the state power is not suspended
in midair. Bonaparte represents a class, and the most numerous class of French society at that, the *small-holding (Parzel-
len) peasants,*"[6] and thus, not only the nonclass of the "Lumpenproletariat!" "The Bonaparte dynasty represents not the
revolutionary, but the conservative peasant. . . . Small-holding
property, in this enslavement by capital to which its development inevitably pushes forward, has transformed the mass of
the French nation into troglodytes. . . . Hence, the peasants
find their natural ally and leader in the *urban proletariat,*
whose task is the overthrow of the bourgeois order."[7] Following these considerations he develops the *"idées Napo-
léoniennes* [which are] *ideas of the undeveloped small holding in the freshness of its youth;* for the small holding that has
outlived its day, they are an absurdity . . . [Napoleon's] contradictory task . . . explains the contradictions of his government,
the confused groping which now seeks to win . . . [but] pro-

duces actual anarchy in the name of order, while at the same time stripping its halo from the entire state machine, profanes it and makes it at once loathsome and ridiculous."[8]

However one may value the historical expositions and point of view, Marx had, in *The Eighteenth Brumaire,* as well as in the essays on the class struggles, delivered masterpieces of political writing. Sombart sensibly and eloquently depicts the lifework of Karl Marx as an artistic one, he speaks of the immense power of his style which comes across despite the rudeness and grossness of his language; Sombart writes: "How he is able to make it fit his special theme! With what passion and intensity the thoughts are developed; what storming stress right to the end of a final line of writing! How the pictures glitter and shine! How the essential nature bubbles and gushes out as from an insatiable spring!" All these characteristics of Marx's writing, which Sombart keenly delineated, can easily be demonstrated by means of passages from the essays on the class struggles, and even more so from the *Brumaire.* But, furthermore, these writings have another everlasting significance: they prove with important examples the applicability and thus, also, the limits of the "materialistic" method. In his introduction to the first essay, Engels wrote in 1894 that he himself had to acknowledge that one can never quite go back to the "final" economic causes in assessing events and series of happenings in daily history; the source of error in trying to assess the changes occurring in the economic condition concurrently as they happen in the historical process is unavoidable. Engels is probably quite right, but he nevertheless rather dogmatically overestimates the method when he calls the economic conditions the actual basis of "all" events. This is something which should have been proved and which cannot be proved; and, Marx had probably not himself understood this.

The Brumaire appeared for the first time in the spring of 1852 as the second number of a monthly journal, which a party member who had settled in New York had tried to publish. It originated under the immediate pressure of events. However, Marx viewed his political writings, like the events from which they originated, as an interruption of his economic studies, which he took up again in London. At first his thoughts were directed primarily to the historical development of national economics, obviously in order to develop his theorems, as well as the necessary consequence of these theorems, in the same manner as Hegel had once depicted his philosophy as the culmination of the history of philosophy. But no publisher was to be found in the Germany of the 1850s for the work, which could have been finished rather quickly at the time. Generally, Engels and Marx, for the time being, were taboo for the reestablished society which conducted itself so self-righteously.

Engels was asked by his father to return home; only reluctantly did he go back to the office in Manchester. Marx suffered greatly in those first years in London, as well as all too often later on. His family was growing; his courageous, industrious wife was not always up to the troubles and hardship of daily life. Engels helped as much as he could, but the thinker, from whom Engels had expected the great new theory of social economic life which was to be the scientific basis of communism had to earn his daily living as a poorly paid wage laborer at a newspaper. He had to be thankful that he was offered employment by the *New York Tribune*, which left him enough energy and time to work on and to advance his favorite and "beloved" work during many years of privation. However, after the preparatory work to the *Critique of the Political Economy* (1859), he merely finished *Capital (Das Kapital),* Volume I, which is usually looked upon as "Marx's Capital." The other parts were published after his death by his friend Engels, and after the latter's death, by Kautsky. Although these parts were far larger in size than the first volume, they did not have a similar influence. Marx's small secondary works will be mentioned later.

Even Marx's political writings, which up to now have only been partially rediscovered, are of scientific character. They necessitated, as he so often complained, an extraordinary splintering of his studies and one has to regret rather deeply that he was not able to direct his talents to either one or the other side exclusively. He was too much a scientist and did, therefore, only "in exceptional cases get involved with the actual newspaper correspondence." It would have been far more fruitful if he had given this rather superficial activity a relatively much smaller part of his time in order to retain a much larger part for science.

In all respects Engels had stood by him, loyal, helpful, and ready to sacrifice. He had always supported Marx's journalistic occupation by word and deed, so that the first essays for the American newspaper about the revolution and counterrevolution in Germany were for the largest part written by Engels (which were translated into German in 1896 and published as Marx's works). However, part of the Marxian works from the *Neue Rheinische Zeitung* newspaper were used as a basis. Later on, Engels, "the general," had contributed, according to his hobby, mostly military articles, and also some parts which were written for an American encyclopedia. In later years Marx also wrote for a few German newspapers which were willing to risk having him write for them. Before this, he had written free contributions to *The People's Paper*, organ of the Chartists which then existed; but the *Tribune* took, by far, the greatest part of his journalistic output.

For this newspaper he watched, with constant readiness and care, according to his way of thinking in reference to world *economic* events, the sphere of English politics and, therefore, world politics. Thus, a number of valuable studies originated, about half of which have been made available to the public through the editorial endeavors of the Russian scholar, N. Rjasanoff. In these studies, the oriental question, and therefore the Crimean War, takes prime consideration; Palmerston's politics are put sharply into focus, Pan-Slavism is comprehended in its fateful meaning, all of its tricks and artifices are laid bare. Much that Marx then stated points out like spotlights the recent events which allowed Pan-Slavism to grow, bloom, and finally rage wildly as the pet-child of the Western Powers, who in 1855–56 were defending Turkey against it.

Marx, the banished, the "Semite," never forgot the fact that he was a German and his duty toward the German people and his fatherland. The American editor of the *Tribune* in 1860 paid him the following tribute; "The only fault I have to find with you, has been that you have occasionally exhibited too German a tone of feeling for an American newspaper. This has been the case with reference both to Russia and France. In questions relating both to Czarism and Bonapartism, I have sometimes thought that you manifested too much interest and too great anxiety for the unity and independence of Germany." This had been evident especially during the Italian War. The editor, Gr. Dana, believed as little as Marx that Italian freedom could be expected from the French emperor, "but I did not think that Germany had any real ground for alarm, as you, in common with other patriotic Germans, thought she had."

At the same time, these contributions of Marx (as well as those of Engels), contained a vast amount of material for a critical, i.e., sociologically based, history of the nineteenth century. Although, of course, they, themselves, are partisans, they nevertheless—due to the fact that their party was at that time quite insignificant and so to say playing a subordinate part —were in a certain sense unprejudiced, impartial onlookers who, with stopwatches in hand, observed the progress and the eventual finish of the happenings as though they were officiating at a fencing event. It would be worth a special book to collect and evaluate those parts of this correspondence which reveal durable truths and those which throw a spotlight on momentary political events. Just to give an example: the summary of the Oriental question on July 19, 1853, reads as follows, "The Czar, vexed and dissatisfied at seeing his immense Empire confined to one sole port of export, and even that situated on a sea unnavigable through one half of the year, and assailable by Englishmen through the other half, is pushing the goal of his ancestors, to get access to the Mediterranean; he is separating, one after the other, the remotest members of the Ottoman Empire from its main body, till at last Constantinople, the heart, must cease to beat. He repeats his periodical invasions as often as he thinks his designs on Turkey endangered by the apparent consolidation of the Turkish government, or by the more dangerous symptoms of self-emancipation manifest amongst the Slavs. Counting on the cowardice and apprehensions of the Western Powers, he bullies Europe, and pushes his demands as far as possible, in order to appear magnanimous afterward, by contenting himself with what he immediately wanted."[9]

Marx furthermore maintains that the humiliation of the reactionary Western governments and their apparent inability to defend the interests of European civilization against Russian offenses will stand in good stead for the revolutionary party.

Among the many essays of the two volumes, the ones about Germany and Pan-Slavism will remain of interest: there we find the nice remark to the effect that the so-called democratic and socialistic form of Pan-Slavism in reality only differentiates itself from the ordinary honest Russian Pan-Slavism through its phraseology and hypocrisy. Notable, furthermore, are the articles about Lord Palmerston, which were printed almost entirely in the Chartist organ, *The People's Paper* in 1853, and which appeared as a book in the English language. Although meant to be a great act of accusation, they are also sharp and brilliant characterization which seeks to give justice to the strong and dazzling aspects of this successful statesman while they lay bare his inner smallness in the contradictions between himself and his politics: "At all times the exploiters could count on his help; on the other hand, he wasted a great deal of talkative magnanimity on the exploited." Marx also wrote a short epilogue about Lord "Firebrand" in 1885 for the *Neue Oder-Zeitung.* Here and there we find a great deal of enlightening material about English political conditions in the two volumes, although they take us only into April 1856. The parties, the cliques, the oligarchy and trade, prosperity and crises, voting corruption, financial frauds, and the whole untruth of parliamentarianism are discussed. Quite often one also finds military questions being discussed which, to be sure, without exception flowed from the pen of Engels.

Engels was actually far more suited for the steady observation of world events and of daily politics than was Marx, by nature the scientist. But Engels had to look after the huckster *(Schacher)* in Manchester. He did not know any other ways besides this necessary evil to promote Marx's scientific works and to prepare for the proletarian revolution. Marx's scientific nature must have always been frustrated, even though articles about outstanding economic events in England and on the

Continent made up a large part of his correspondence. He must have been frustrated because, as he put it in January 1859, it was always necessary for him to "acquaint himself with the practical details which lay outside the realm of the actual science of economics." After the interruption of the previous years, he took up his economic studies again in London in 1850. "The immense material for the history of the political economy, which lies piled up in the British Museum, the favorable position which London affords for the observation of bourgeois society, and finally the new developmental stage into which bourgeois society seemed to have entered since the discovery of gold in Australia and California,—all these make it mandatory that I start again from the beginning, and that I work myself through the new material quite critically."

The clear result of these vast labors is available at the end of that phase of his life which is here under consideration. But besides the first volume of *Capital*, of which a first rough draft was published in 1859, the man of unrelenting industriousness had, in these years, despite the above-mentioned obstacles, written, "in widely spaced periods," a whole series of monographs "for his own better understanding, but not for publication." For the comprehensive elaboration of this huge amount of material he had an equally gigantic plan. He wanted to analyze the whole system of "bourgeois economics" in the following order: capital, landed property, wage labor, the state, foreign trade, and the world market. Later on, he restricted his plan to the first of the six categories and wanted to investigate capital in three great parts: at first, the process of production, then the process of circulation, then the total process. The history of the development of the theory was then to follow.

The four volumes of correspondence between Marx and Engels, in which Mrs. Marx also takes part, gives us a glimpse into Marx's burdensome daily life—into the development of his studies, into the manifold kinds of other activities besides his political journalism. According to the nature of things, the exchange of letters is especially lively as long as Engels lived in Manchester (until 1871); later on the correspondence is revived, whenever Marx had to spend time at health spas, which his many ills made mandatory and which trips were possible through his improved economic situation. Also, after Engels became independent he was able to help financially more than before.

The "emigration," the name by which the pitiful group of revolutionary refugees in the London of the fifties called themselves, soon showed morbid traits: quarrels, dissensions, wordy manifestoes, distress, and demoralization. Marx and Engels (the latter had just moved from London to Manchester in November 1850) tried very hard at first to stem this decay. They wanted to reconcile the League of Communists with the London Central Committee, but then in September 1850 dissension broke out within the latter. Marx accused the die-hards of sanctifying the word "proletariat." He goes on to say: "We tell the workers, you have fifteen, twenty, even twenty-five years of civil war and other strife to go through, not only in order to effect a change in the conditions, but to change yourselves so that you may be capable of political government; but you say to the contrary: we must govern at once or we can all go to sleep." The break was abrupt. Some months later Marx wrote, "I am quite pleased with the public isolation wherein the two of us, you and I, now find ourselves. It is quite in accordance with our position and our principles." With distaste he talked about the bombastic manifestoes which were being sent into the world at that time by the defeated revolutionaries: French, Italians, Poles, Hungarians, and Germans. Some friends felt alienated from Marx because of the bitter critique which he wrote about Gottfried Kinkel's defense speech (August 7, 1849) in the last volume of his *Neue Rheinische Zeitung*.

Marx indeed remained alone in London; one of his loyal friends was Ferdinand Freiligrath, who, more poet than politician, had found a good management position in a banking agency. In the first years there was still lingering political excitement because of the lawsuit against communists in Cologne, which took place in October 1852, and which ended in a heavy defeat for the Prussian police. Marx was successful in proving that the main piece of evidence of Stieber, a supposedly existing original protocol book of the Marxian party, was a monstrous forgery. The disclosure and resulting polemic against the conspiratory and revolutionary alliance of the former comrades, Willich and Schapper, cost Marx labor and mental energy. The Communist League had now dissolved completely, and Marx was glad to be able to return to his scientific endeavors. In 1853 he complained about how the steady journalistic work was boring him: "It takes far too much time, dissipates, and still amounts to nothing." However, he must have been glad to be freed of the revolutionary fraternities.

The letters to Engels of the first years testify of Marx's detailed studies on monetary theory. Through a German publishing house he tried to publish a large manuscript on the development of theories about money and capital, but this fell through. It is remarkable that he devoted so much attention, even in 1851, to the writings of Proudhon, namely his *Idée générale de la Révolution au XIXième siècle,* from which he wrote very extensive excerpts to Engels, also exchanging his thoughts on this with the latter. Marx also wanted to have this critique on Proudhon published in Germany, but this goal could not be attained either. In the meanwhile, he also "ground" away in the British Museum, mainly on technology, its history, and agronomy, "to get at least an idea of that stuff." The World Fair, which took place in London in 1851, lent him a good number of inspirations for this task.

Engels said at this time that it would be the most important thing for Marx to present a big book to the public, and the best, because the least disputed, topic would be history. Engels thought that it was absolutely necessary that the spell be broken, which had been occasioned by the long absence of Marx from the book market, and by the fear of the bookstores that his books would not sell. However, in the meantime, Marx's attention was drawn to the agitation about Louis Napoleon's coup d'état and the economic and political events which followed this. Finally, a first draft of his life's work was ready for the publisher. With the help of Lassalle the little booklet *"Zur Kritik der politischen Ökonomie"* ("On the Critique of Political Economy") was printed in Berlin by Franz Duncker.

Around this time Mrs. Marx wrote to an old party comrade

in America: "The Moor" (this was a nickname of her husband as father of the family; some of his friends also made use of it) is quite on top of things; his whole former work capacity and easiness at work has returned, just as the freshness and serenity of his intellect, which "had been broken for years," she added, "since that great pain, the loss of the child of our heart, for whom my heart will eternally be sad." This refers to the greatest sorrow which befell their family life, so plagued and tried: the death of a boy who had been the sunshine of the house.

Soon after the little book had appeared, the researcher and thinker had to get busy once again with one of the "plants" which the "immigration manure" (as he sometimes expressed it) had brought forth: the defense against Karl Vogt, the democrat of the Paulskirche, who had now become a very famous materialistic natural scientist in Geneva.

In the preceding years between 1854 and 1859, the Marx-Engels letter-exchange is very much concerned with political events in connection with their obligations in writing for newspapers. However, their exchange of views, especially on historical subjects, goes far beyond the concerns of the day. For a long time these discussions dealt with the Crimean War, especially of course, the attitude of the English government and English public opinion. In between, there was trouble with the *New York Tribune*, which did not treat Marx very well at all; then, much deeper, the great sorrow about the loss of his boy in April 1855. Six days after the event Marx wrote to Engels, "In all the terrible sorrows which I have had to go through in these days, the thought about you and your friendship has kept me going, and the hope that we will still have something sensible together in the world to do."

For a time in 1857, the two were busy with the plan of an American encyclopedia to which both were supposed to contribute; and special interest had been expressed for the military articles of Engels. But then the great money crisis of 1857 took their sharpest attention, and once again they were under the illusion that the great proletarian revolution would follow thereupon, even though Engels complained that the long prosperity had been terribly demoralizing (December 17, 1857). Also, the revolt in India rather disturbingly made headlines.

We find many traces of the great scientific and literary eagerness characteristic of both revolutionaries. At one time as he was leafing through Hegel's Logic, Marx showed great enthusiasm to work out, in two or three printed pages "if there should ever be time for such work again,"[10] the rationale of the method which Hegel had discovered, but at the same time mystified, so that this method would be made comprehensible to common sense. One may remember that this very same thought returned some fifteen years later in the "Preface" to the second edition of *Capital.* Receiving Lassalle's work on Heraclitus *(Die Philosophie Herakleiton des Dunklen)* also led Marx back to philosophy. He judged the book of rather poor quality and said that although Lassalle was boasting when asserting that Heraclitus had up to then been an unknown personality, a book with seven seals, he, Lassalle, nevertheless, had added absolutely nothing new to what Hegel had already stated in his *History of Philosophy.*

When they discussed economic problems, then Engels with his practical business experience had to help. A year before the small booklet "To the Critique" *("Zur Kritik")* was published, Marx told his friend in very great detail about his plan of work on *Capital.* Engels very hesitantly answered to the effect that he found it rather difficult to detect the dialectical connections because *all abstract reasoning* had become very foreign to him. At that time Engels was busy with physiology and comparative anatomy, but he thought the organic cell was the Hegelian "to-be-in-itself" (An-sich-sein) and followed in its development exactly the Hegelian process, until in the end the finished organism had developed from it. This philosophical letter crossed in the mail a very sad letter of Marx's about his economic needs, which he closed with an expression of his deep anger that his intellect was being ruined with rubbish and that his capacity to work was being broken. Extensive accounting of his expenditures accompanied this outburst. As always, Engels helped as well as he could.

Soon there were other political events, namely the Italian War of 1859, which again deterred Marx from his economic studies. One is continually amazed that the thinker took so much time for his letter-exchanges, despite his serious difficul-

ties. Many personal notes are included in these letters, as for
instance, on the visit of Bruno Bauer and the latter's literary
plans (the old polemic did not shatter the still older friendship
between these two), on letters from Johannes Miquel and Ferdinand Lassalle, as well as information about the friendship
with Ferdinand Freiligrath and Wilhelm Liebknecht. In January 1860, Marx thought it might very well be possible that a
new war would break out even before the beginning of that
summer. The international circumstances were so complicated that it was of the utmost importance for vulgar
democracy and liberalism "to cut us off from the ear of the
German philistines (i.e., the German public) and from having
access to them." This referred to the case of Vogt. Marx saw
himself forced to defend the alleged band of hooligans
(Schwefelbande) in London: Vogt had collected a great
amount of gossip about the ostensible followers of Marx, which
cost Marx much time and effort to expose as a defamation.
Nevertheless, he worked on *Capital* during 1860, and he
thought at one point that he was going to have it—he meant
apparently the first volume—finished in about six weeks' time.

But new hindrances, one after another, came his way. World
events would not leave him in peace. After the Italian War,
which was the topic of two brochures by Engels, "Rivers Po
and Rhine," and "Savoy, Nice and the Rhine," a much more
important event followed—the American Civil War. This, in
turn, was followed by the liberation of Schleswig-Holstein and
then by the German War of 1866, signaling the end of the
German Confederation. All were exciting events for the two
valiant revolutionaries. In the American cause, Marx took the
position of the North much more decisively than did Engels,
that is, against the position of Palmerston as chief of the English, and of Louis Napoleon as chief of the French bourgeoisie,
who were in favor of the slaveholders. Marx soon believed he
recognized that, in the same manner as the American War of
Independence of the eighteenth century had rung the alarm
bell for the European middle classes, so the Civil War of the
nineteenth century would ring the bell for the European
working classes. Furthermore, the German question and its
forceful solution through Bismarck caught the anxious atten-

tion of the two. Engels, whose military knowledge often stood him in good stead, nevertheless, was wrong in his estimation of the Austrians, as well as of the American southern states. He did not want the Prussians to be successful and, therefore, was rather surprised by the events. But when the fighting was over, Marx and Engels were realistic enough not to side with the conquered, but rather to see these events as a necessary phase of progress.

Even more significant than these events for Marx's personality and activities were the new stirrings within the European workers' movement, which pulled him into their circles during these years. With the demise of the Communist League, Marx had "systematically"—so he wrote in a letter in 1864—refused all participation in any organization. At times Lassalle had tried to involve him in his plans, and when, in the year 1861, Marx was amnestied and could travel back into Germany, Lassalle proposed to him that they found a newspaper in the Prussian capital. However, nothing ever came of it. Marx did not like Lassalle, although the latter honored Marx as his master. Engels was of the same opinion as his friend. Both had a very poor estimation of Lassalle's character and not a better one of his philosophic-scientific achievements. So they could only meet with distrust the great agitation which Lassalle initiated in the spring of 1863 in the German worker class. Lassalle's way of thinking simply was not theirs. In the confidential letters between the two, one finds strong expressions —as much about Lassalle's theoretical shortcomings as about his unbridled vanity. This had to do with the fact that in 1861 Marx was Lassalle's guest in Berlin, and that in the following year, Lassalle visited the Marx household for a number of weeks, which was a very heavy burden on the household budget for Jenny (Mrs. Marx), because Marx's economic situation in those years was worse than it had ever been before. But Engels helped tirelessly. Lassalle's death in 1864, nevertheless, shook both of them. But the reason for his death—the duel with a "dismissed rival who, besides being a rival, was also a Wallachian swindler" as Engels put it—Marx calls just one of the many indiscretions which Lassalle had committed during his life. He was convinced that, had Lassalle not been in the

vicinity of *military adventurers* and *révolutionnaires en gants
jaunes* in Switzerland, this catastrophe would not have happened. "But it was fate that continually compelled him to go
to this Koblenz of the European revolution."

On the other hand, Marx was very glad that he had with-
stood the incitements from various sides and had never attacked the great agitator during his "jubilee year." However,
in his letters, he had criticized these agitations severely
enough: Lassalle assumed an air of importance, using phrases
borrowed from Marx and Engels, conducting himself as
though he were a future worker-dictator. Marx took special
offence at Lassalle's continuous boastings; he had stopped his
letter-exchange with him since the beginning of that year.
When Marx later credited Lassalle with the immortal merit of
having reawakened the German workers' movement after
fifteen years of sleep, one must remember that at the time the
friends looked upon this movement, too, with distrust. However, after Lassalle's death in October 1864, an event at first
seemingly unimportant, had for the two, and especially for
Marx, a far-reaching significance: This was the founding of the
Working Men's International Association.

Marx comments on this in a long letter to Friedrich on
November 4, 1864, in which he encloses many exhibits which
he numbers "in order not to forget what I wanted to tell you."
Number 1 treats "Lassalle and the Countess Hatzfeld"; the
latter had complained to Liebknecht that Marx had neglected
Lassalle. Marx writes: "as if I could have been of more service
to the man than to keep quite and let him go ahead." Number
2 follows the theme specified as *"Working Men's International
Association."* "Some time ago the London workers had sent an
address about Poland to the Paris workers and summoned
them to joint action in this matter. The Parisians on their part
sent over a deputation headed by a worker called *Tolvin, the
real worker's candidate at the last election in Paris,* a very nice
fellow. (His companions, too, were quite nice lads.)"[11] There
was a meeting on September 28, 1864, in St. Martin's Hall,
arranged by members at the English trade unions and the
masons' union. A young Frenchman had been sent to Marx to
express the wish that he should send a German worker as

speaker to the meeting and that he should participate for the German workers. Marx stated that it was a standing rule with him to refuse such invitations. He had in this case, however, made an exception because he knew that from the London side, as well as from the Paris side, real "powers" were represented. (He had put the word in quotation marks himself and at the same time he remarked that a resurgence of the working class was noticeable.) Hence, Karl Marx attended the meeting "which was packed to suffocation." He brought along with him the tailor Eccarius who served as a speaker and who did a very fine job. Marx was also "present as a mute figure on the platform!" Both men were elected to be part of the provisional committee; moreover, Marx was elected to the committee which was to formulate the guiding theses. Apparently, the participants, or instigators, of the meeting were no strangers to Marx's importance. He writes in some detail about those first meetings, one of which was in his own house. He soon realized, however, that if not already, he was soon to become the intellectual leader of the union.

He designed an "inaugural address," which was not accepted without strong opposition by the subordinate committee, but was accepted by the general committee unanimously and with great enthusiasm. His address depicts the depressed condition of the working class in Europe in contrast to the intoxicating epoch of progressive national wealth; it points an accusing finger toward the even quicker return, the constantly enlarging circle, and deathly effects of that social pest called industrial and commercial crisis; it bewails the joint defeat of the British and the Continental working classes after the failure of the Revolution of 1848. Nevertheless, Marx states the development is not without its brighter side, for two great events stand out: first, the ten-hour law in England—"The immense physical, moral and intellectual benefits hence accruing to the factory operative, semiannually chronicled in the reports of the inspectors of factories, are now acknowledged on all sides."[12] That law was the victory of a principle, that principle being the control of social production through social insight and foresight over the blind dominance of the law of supply and demand. "It was the first time that in broad daylight the political economy of the middle class succumbed to the political economy of the working class."[13] But an even greater victory was awaiting the working class, and this was the second great event. "We speak of the cooperative movement, especially the cooperative factories raised by the unassisted efforts of a few bold 'hands.' The value of these great social experiments cannot be overrated. By deed, instead of by argument, they have shown that production on a large scale, and in accord with the behests of modern science, may be carried on without the existence of a class of masters employing a class of hands . . . and that, like slave labor, and serf labor, hired labor is but a transitory and inferior form, destined to disappear before associated labor plying its toil with a willing hand, a ready mind, and a joyous heart."[14]

The limits of the effectiveness of the cooperative system, whose seeds had been sown by Robert Owen, are outlined: the conclusion follows that to free the working masses, there must be development in the national heirarchy and assistance through national means. The bounden duty of the working classes is now to acquire political power. "They seem to have comprehended this, for in England, Germany, Italy, and France, there have taken place simultaneous revivals of and simultaneous efforts are being made at the political reorganization of the working men's party."[15]

The address ends with the command that the working classes should penetrate into the secrets of international politics, and see to the propagation of the idea that the simple laws of morality and right, which underlie the relationship between private persons also be made to hold for the uppermost laws governing the relations between nations. The struggle for this form of foreign politics is included in the general struggle for the emancipation of the working class. The last words of his speech repeat the motto of the *Communist Manifesto:* Proletarians of all countries, unite!

Even though the acceptance of the new *Manifesto* meant a great success for the German scholar, who for so many years had held himself aloof from involvement in practical movements, Marx, nevertheless, was not deceived about the difficulty in achieving his ideas in this circle. He recognized that it was necessary to proceed *suaviter in modo;* time would be needed until the rekindled movement would allow the old keenness of language to reassert itself. For it was not true at all, as Wilhelm Liebknecht said in 1896, that Marx had been responsible for calling the First International into existence—Marx's participation was hesitant and almost against his will. The core of the Association was formed by British unionists, with whom a few old Owenites and Chartists had associated themselves, together with a small group of learned Comtists, as well as French Proudhonists whose theories and phrases Marx thoroughly despised. He was asked to support the tactics of the unions, and in the endeavor to imbue them with some general ideas and political spirit; he met with the Comtists, to whom he felt philosophically superior. Nevertheless, there were friendly connections with union leaders, as well as with a positivist, a professor of history, Spencer-Beesly, who had presided at the Association meeting in St. Martin's Hall. It was sad, however, that the work for this organization took so much time of the thinker and researcher. The conclusion of his first volume, on which he had worked especially hard in the year 1863, was also interrupted many times by his many physical ailments, and it was now delayed anew. The International Association, "and all that goes with it," was pressing like a nightmare upon him (from a letter dated December 26, 1865). Therefore, he must have welcomed the opportunity to give the newly won public, which did look up to him with much respect but very little knowledge, an insight into his theory. This was possible through a speech Marx gave in June 1865 in the General Assembly ("Wages, Price, and Profit"—a German translation has recently been made available). It is based on a polemic against the old Owenite, Weston, who, in the *Beehive* (a paper, at times serving as an organ of the International Association), untiringly defended the proposition that a general increase of wages would not be of much avail to the laborer, and that, therefore, the unions were having a detrimental effect. In thoroughly contradicting these views, Marx concludes that a general increase of workers' wages could "by and large" not influence the price of goods, but would only work toward the lowering of profit, while the general tendency of the capitalistic mode of production was directed at lowering the average normal wage. The unions would, therefore, be effective as centers of opposition against this tendency. But, he continues, "they fail partially from an injudicious use of their power. They fail generally from limiting themselves to a guerrilla war against the effects of the existing system, instead of simultaneously trying to change it, instead of using their organized forces as a lever for the final emancipation of the working class, that is to say, the ultimate abolition of the wages system."[16] In September 1865 the first "Conference" of the International was held in London. Among other things, it passed the resolution to fight for the restoration of an independent Poland "on a democratic basis" and accepted the motion that the agenda of the Constituent Congress should include the religious idea as related to the social, political, and intellectual development. This Constituent Congress was held from September 3–8, 1866, in Geneva, the city which had become the center of the organization through Johann Philipp Becker's newspaper, *Der Vorbote*.

Marx did not participate in this Congress, although he spent much time in the arrangements for it. He was working on the conclusion to his book and declared in a confidential letter that, according to him, what he could personally do at any one congress was far less important than what he was doing through his endeavors for the working classes. He was satisfied with the result of the Congress. After powerful struggles, his direction had gained the majority (the English memorandum was written by him). However, "the ignorant talkativeness of the French annoyed him." This is easy to comprehend in that the French and with them Proudhonism had control at the Second Congress held at Lausanne from September 2–8.

Marx did not attend this Congress either. But his book did finally see the light of day: *Das Kapital. Kritik der Politischen Oekonomie Erster Band. Buch I: Der Producktionsprozess des Kapitals.* [*Capital—A Critique of the Political Economy. First Volume, Book One: The Production Process of Capital.*] Much more than just this first book was ready, or nearly ready, but the material was not in order; the editors still had a lot to do on these manuscripts. On February 16, 1866, Marx himself had written, "Although it is ready, the manuscript is only middling in its present form, it cannot be published by anyone except myself, not even by you [Engels]." Excessive nightwork was then the cause of much of his ill health. Also political excitement due to the German War proved to be a hindrance. In November the first parcel of manuscripts finally went to Otto Meissner in Hamburg, Germany; five months later, the author himself brought the remaining ones to Hamburg. The sea journey was beneficial to his health. In connection with this trip he had visited an admirer, the gynecologist, Dr. Kugelmann, in Hannover, who had urgently invited him. He found here that he (and Engels) had a larger influence on educated civil servants than on the workers. He was told that he could count on the visit of Bennigsen, but whether or not it ever took place is not known. In May he returned to London. The manuscript was printed in Leipzig. By August, Marx had corrected the final page. "Finally, this volume is ready." He wrote to Engels, "I owe it to you alone that this was at all possible. Without your sacrificing for me, I could never have made the vast effort necessary for the three volumes." In the same vein he had written from Hannover that it had always been on his conscience, "that you [Engels] squandered your splendid powers and let them rust for my sake." It was his intention to get the other two volumes ready for the following spring.

NOTES AND REFERENCES

Translators' Note: Although no page numbers are given, the many unacknowledged quotations are from Marx and Engels, *Selected Correspondence*.

1. T.N.: Marx and Engels, *Selected Works* (Moscow: Foreign Languages Publishing House, 1962), vol. I, p. 137. Hereafter abbreviated to S W I.
1a. T.N.: Ibid., p. 146.
2. T.N.: Ibid., p. 163.
3. T.N.: Ibid., p. 171.
4. T.N.: Ibid., p. 224.
4a. T.N.: Ibid., p. 308.
5. T.N.: Ibid., pp. 323–24.
6. T.N.: Ibid., pp. 329–33.
7. T.N.: Ibid., pp. 335–38.
8. T.N.: Ibid., pp. 340–44.
9. *New York Tribune*, August 5, 1853.
10. T.N.: Marx and Engels, *Selected Correspondence 1843–1895* (Moscow: Foreign Language Publishing House, no publication date), p. 179. Hereafter designated as M E S C.
11. T.N.: Ibid.
12. T.N.: S W I 382.
13. T.N.: Ibid., p. 383.
14. T.N.: Ibid.
15. T.N.: Ibid., p. 384.
16. T.N.: Ibid., p. 447.

Chapter 4

UP TO HIS DEATH (1867–1883)

Marx was to live still another fifteen and one-half years, but his work remained unfinished, unordered, and, if one excludes the small circle of followers and admirers, misunderstood. Yet this work in three volumes, to which he intended to add the history of the theory, was supposed to be only the first of six works which were to comprise the whole system! Marx had witnessed only the second edition of the first volume and had written an important Preface *(Vorrede)* to it in 1873. A year earlier Russian and French translations had been printed, in which Marx himself had collaborated, incorporating a number of changes. However, it was impossible for him to bring out an English translation, although he and Engels tried very hard to do so. But this first—the only, but a giant volume—has started its path through the world literature and the ground trembles under its steps. What was edited (posthumously) is not of the same strength, but, nevertheless, it is stamped with Marx's intellect.

The work for the International progressed and consisted in the main of a very far-flung correspondence. The Third Congress was held in Brussels in September 1868. Here the Russian, Bakunin, whom Marx had known in Paris in 1843, stood out. Soon Bakunin became the center of a strong opposition directed against Marx. The significance of the International was steadily advanced in these years through a number of large worker strikes, in which the International itself was supposedly involved.

The writer remembers from his own youth that, at that time, the International was making its appearance as the incarnation of the red ghost: newspapers were filled with hints pointing at its secret powers, its unlimited financial means, and Karl Marx appeared as the sinister leader of a worldwide conspiracy. This was only an apparition, because in reality, the International was a slow-moving organization, which took on a different character in each country where it was established, but everywhere it had to fight hard for money and support and against indifference, notwithstanding the fact that the influence of both men was slowly increasing. Marx was the corresponding secretary of the "Generalrat" (General Council) for Germany and Holland, and Engels held the same office for Spain. It was characteristic of this fragmentation, under which the worker movement was still suffering, that the general German workers' union *(Allgemeine Deutsche Arbeiterverein)* led by Herr von Schweitzer was not a member of the International.

The International's most important Congress was held in Basel in 1869. Again, Marx did not participate in the Congress, but spiritually he was there through a report of the General Council (about the right of inheritance) which he had written. Marx thought it rather absurd and in poor taste to look upon the abolition of the right of inheritance as the starting point for a social revolution. However, Bakunin, who had more adherents, opposed Marx on this matter, and a decision could not be reached; rather, it was decided that society had the right to transform the soil and ground into communal property, and that this transformation would be necessary in the interest of society. These decisions aroused fear throughout the world. Shortly afterward the German-French War broke out. Of course, Marx and Engels followed it with interest. The final result—that the Germans would be victorious—was, in the last days of July, a certainty for Engels who had on his own designed the Prussian military campaign. In an address to the General Council, which was praised by John Stuart Mill and other intellectuals, Marx declared the war a German war of defense, but at the same time accused the Prussians and Bismarck of neglecting to present a neighboring free Germany to an enslaved France. "In the background of this suicidal struggle Russia, the assassin, lies in ambush."[1] On August 15 Engels judged that Bismarck was now doing, as in 1866, "a piece of our work"[2]; in his own way and quite unintentionally, he was clearing the way for their ideas. Engels states that if Liebknecht's opinion that one should remain neutral were the general opinion in Germany "we would soon have the Confederation of the Rhine (Rheinbund) again, and the honorable Wilhelm (Liebknecht) should then see what kind of a role he would play in it and where the worker movement would be."[3] The one sentence which has become so meaningful today then follows: "A folk which is always beaten and trampled upon is indeed the true folk to stage a revolution—especially so in Wilhelm's (Liebknecht's) beloved small states."[4]

At the time Marx was already worried about the province of Alsace-Lorraine and the craving for it, which seemed to be predominant in two circles: in the Prussian court circles and the south German Beer-Patriotism. "It [the annexation of Alsace-Lorraine] would be the severest misfortune which could befall Europe and specifically Germany."[5] Engels was convinced that Bismarck would have concluded peace arrangements, without asking for the transfer of territory, had a revolutionary government appeared on the scene at the right time. After the victory of Sedan he said: "the Alsace swindle" was, besides the basic Teutonic element in it, mainly of a strategic nature and, that Bismarck needed the German-speaking part of Lorraine up to the Vosges Mountains as a buffer zone. Marx had previously maintained that the Prussians should have learned from their own history that one cannot obtain "eternal" security from a conquered opponent through "dismemberment." The "horse cure of Tilsit" was not advantageous to Napoleon I. One finds these thoughts reiterated in the second address to the General Council on September 9, which, with some satisfaction, repeats the sentiments found in the first one, namely: "The death knell for the Second Empire has already tolled in Paris."[6] He also warned in the speech, "If the German working class allows the present war to give up its strictly defensive character, and to change into a war against the French nation, then victory or defeat will be equally disastrous."[7] After presenting the military reasons for annexation of Alsace and German-Lorraine, he states that it is illogical and anachronistic to elevate these military reasons into a principle by which to determine the national borders: Prussia to act against France like Napoleon I acted against Prussia. *"The end will be no less disastrous this time."* . . . Germany is either

going to be the obvious slave of Russian aggrandizement, or it
will have to prepare again, after a short rest, for a new defensive war . . . for a racial war against the united races of the Slavs
and the Romance peoples. . . . Do the Germanophiles really
believe that freedom and peace are secure in Germany when
they push France into the arms of Russia?[8] The speech, it may
be noted, welcomed the French Republic.

The consecutive historic events were the winter offensive,
the bombardment and the starving of Paris, the capitulation,
the revolt of the Commune and its defeat. Of all the events,
the last must have most angered the old rebels. After the end
of the revolt, Marx prepared an address in the name of the
General Council about the "Civil War in France"; it carried
the date of May 30, 1871. The old energy for the presentation
of current events is fully alive in this address. Although the
International did not have any influence on the formation and
composition of the Commune and only little influence on the
measures taken by the Commune during its short life span—
the majority was composed of Blanquists, the minority of
Proudhonists, among them were a few members of the Association—Marx, nevertheless, defended their actions so vigor-
ously that even his own followers, especially those in England,
were shocked. He even defended the execution of the sixty-
four hostages, which included the Archbishop of Paris. He said
their lives had been forfeited again and again because of the
steady killing of captured soldiers by the Versailles people.
"The real murderer of Bishop Derboy is Thiers."[9] The heads
of government of national defense were depicted as moral
monsters. The proclamation originated under the immediate
influence which the terrible cruelty, vindictiveness, and anger
of the victors, defeated shortly before, must have made on any
sensitive person, but especially on the advocate of the working
class. The proclamation seethes with righteous and moral indignation and is intended to defend the honor of the Commu-
nards. With noble intentions it takes upon itself the responsibility for deeds in which the International itself had no part.
Marx very strongly holds the notion that the Commune had
been essentially a government of the working classes, the
finally found political form under which the economic libera-

tion of the workers could occur; it should have become the lever to overthrow the economic basis on which the existence of the classes, and thus the dominance of one class, is resting; only thereby could the Communal constitution have become something other than an impossibility and a deception. The Commune was to create its own conditions for existence out of itself! Although Marx had always taught that these conditions for each new society would be hatched in the womb of the old one preceding it.

The Commune, as well as the war which preceded it, became fateful for the International. Discord within the groups increased, and the much-desired fraternity and peacefulness waned especially under Bakunin's intrigues. *Bakunin* was an aristocratic Russian, a revolutionary more out of a wild passion than from any theoretical conviction, a real desperado; he had founded a special alliance within the International. In a letter dated November 23, 1871, Marx characterized his program as a mixture superficially gathered together from right and left, ideas consisting of equality of the classes (after which Marx puts an exclamation mark), the abolition of the right of inheritance as the starting point of the social movement (Marx labels this a St. Simonistic nonsense), atheism dictated as dogma for the members, and as main dogma (Proudhonistic) abstinence from political action.

Shortly before Marx wrote this letter, a closed conference, which the General Council had called, was held in London. Although it was sparsely attended, some important resolutions were passed, especially in regard to "sects and amateur groups." By these resolutions, Marx made the General Council, that is, himself, the governor of the International. However, it was too late—the division could no longer be prevented. The word had been passed—according to Marx, it was the ragged part of the French refugees in Geneva and London who were behind it—that in the General Council, Teutonism (i.e., Bismarckism) was the order of the day. "This refers to the unforgivable fact that I am originally a German and that indeed I have exerted a decisive intellectual influence upon the General Council." Numerically, Marx says, the German element is much weaker than the English or the French. The sin

is in the fact that the German element dominated *theoretically*
and that this dominance—that is, German science—had been
found quite useful and even indispensable by the non-Ger-
mans. Notwithstanding this position of power which he had
gained, Marx, nevertheless, had to doubt the ability of the
International to continue to exist. However, he was willing to
call once more the annual Congress, which met on September
2 in The Hague. Marx participated personally. He knew very
well that this Congress determined the life or death of the
International. He himself gave it the death sentence when he
followed the suggestion made by Engels to transfer the General Council from London to New York. This motion was
passed by a small majority. Furthermore, the Congress barred
Bakunin and his follower, Guillaume, from the International.

For a short while the International vegetated. According to
Marx, the Congress held at Geneva in 1873 was a fiasco. It was
indeed the last sign of life of the first International. The dis-
agreement with Bakunin was concluded by a memorandum
which has become known under the German title, *A Complot
Against the International Working Men's Association.* Finally,
the year 1877 witnessed the International's formal end. Bakunin died in the same year, after having been very active sowing
the seeds of anarchy which were sprouting sporadically in
Russia, in the Romance countries, and even in the United
States.

It is not certain what reasons were instrumental in Marx's
giving up his interest in the International. His intercession for
the Commune had alienated him from the leading English
unionists as much as it had made the French suspicious of him.
Although he was opposed to Bismarck, he did not want to deny
the German in him; moreover, he was quite aware how much
the immensely strenuous and rarely gratifying work for the
Association had become a serious hindrance for his intellectual
lifework, which he was still hoping to complete.

While the International Working Men's Association, which
had been called into life with such great hope and which
through Marx's energy had been brought to the fore, almost
against his will, was disappearing without fanfare; the German
Social Democratic Party was growing rapidly, greatly assisted

by the general rise of the German nation. A group of Marxists, called "Eisenacher" or "Ehrliche" (honest ones) under the leadership of Wilhelm Liebknecht, competed with the followers of Lassalle. Liebknecht, although a constant house guest of the Marx family in his London exile, was rejected by both Marx and Engels as a politician because of his all-German, thus anti-Prussian, inclinations. They, like Liebknecht, hated Lassalle and mistrusted the latter's successor, Herr von Schweitzer. But Liebknecht had succeeded in winning Bebel for the cause, and in this one personality the London chiefs perceived the future of the party. The Lassallean and Eisenach factions were feuding strongly. The persecution and oppression of both groups, especially by state prosecutors, forged the two opposing parties together which since February 1875 had been negotiating unification. Marx gave the draft of a proposed unified program a very sharp critique in a letter which only became publicly known in 1890. He saw in the draft far too much of Lassalle and too little of, or only falsified, Marx in it. Nevertheless, the unification took place in May 1875 at the Congress of Gotha. The newly founded Socialistic Worker Party of Germany grew in the following years, despite the setbacks caused by the great economic crisis which was besetting the victorious German nation, as well as the whole of the industrialized world, after the soar of the "Gründerära" (between 1871 and 1874). Several attempts on the life of the German emperor crudely highlighted the gloominess of the general situation and terrified all peaceful citizens. The leading German statesman of the time (Bismarck) thought it best to subdue the publicly dangerous aspirations of social democracy by means of an exceptional law. He used this opportunity to assure himself a majority in the Reichstag for his new customs policy. This repression was succeeded by the workers' insurance bill, but Bismarck until the very end of his career was completely opposed to any extension of the workers' insurance protection.

We have little evidence how the march of events affected Marx, because the correspondence with Engels ceased to be regular when Engels settled in London, where they lived close to each other. We know sufficiently well, however, especially from letters directed to a party comrade named Sorge living in New York, that Marx, as well as Engels, was quite dissatisfied with developments. Characteristic is the outburst in which he, in October 1877, still damns the compromise with the Lassalleans which had led to other compromises with such underlings as Dühring in Berlin and his "admirers," and also with a whole gang of "half-ripe" students and "overwise" doctors who wanted to give socialism a higher idealistic turn. That is, they wanted to replace its materialistic basis (which calls for serious objective study if one wishes to operate on it) with a modern mythology with its goddesses of justice, freedom, equality, and *fraternité*. Marx and Engels denied the joint cooperation of the new socialistic papers, *Die Zukunft*, which was published in Berlin, and *Die Neue Gesellschaft*, published in Zurich. On September 4, 1878, Marx, writing about the law against the socialists, said merely: "Mr. Bismarck works very well for us." There are indications that he regarded this law as a wholesome crisis for the party. At the same time, he viewed with satisfaction the total European development. His teachings were progressing in France under the influence of *Guesdés* and of Marx's son-in-law, *Lafargue*. It was gratifying for him that Englishmen such as *John Rae, Hyndman, Belfort-Bax* had started to look seriously at *Capital*. It was natural that Marx was very much moved by the extraordinarily large success which Henry George's work, *Progress and Poverty*, had gained in the United States, and from there also in Europe. It was natural, too, that Marx found George quite behind the times as an economist, although he recognized the first attempt of this American to free himself from orthodox political economics. He saw the practical suggestion that ground rent should be paid to the state, only as a short-term measure, which, as such, was already suggested in the *Manifesto*, although it was in itself contradictory. Nonetheless, he respected George as a writer with talent.

Marx's economic condition improved in his later years by virtue of the fact that the loyal Engels was in the position to assure him a steady income (250 pounds per annum). He was happy to see two of his daughters married to Frenchmen whom he esteemed, Paul Lafargue and Charles Longuet. However, his health waned; and for three successive years (from 1874 on) he took a good cure in Karlsbad, and in the following year in Neuenahr. The law against the socialists ended these spa-journeys. He was especially hard hit in his personal life by the incurable illness of his wife beginning in the fall of 1879, and ending with her death on December 2, 1881. His own health was equally affected; he had a chronic bronchitis infection, and was all the more shaken by the loss of his wife. While he was visiting the Isle of Wight, where he went in the spring of 1882 according to his doctor's recommendation, he contracted pleurisy. He moved from there to Algiers, where he had a setback, then via Monte Carlo to Paris and Argenteuil, to his daughter, Mrs. Longuet; finally, he spent another six weeks with his daughter Laura on Lake Geneva in Vevey. In September 1882, he returned to London with a new will to live, but a new fate broke his last powers—the sudden death of his oldest daughter, Jenny Longuet. He returned from the funeral with a new case of bronchitis, and a developing abscess in the lung caused a rapid loss of powers. He died on March 14, 1883, quietly and without pain.

Engels, still under the fresh impression of events, wrote the following day to Sorge: "Medical skill might have been able to assure him a few more years of vegetative existence, the life of a helpless being. Our Marx, however, would never have borne that. To live, with all the unfinished works before him, tantalized by the desire to complete them and unable to do so, would have been a thousand times more bitter to him than the gentle death that overtook him. 'Death is not a misfortune to him who dies, but to him who survives,' he used to say, quoting Epicurus. And to see this mighty genius lingering on as a physical wreck for the greater glory of medicine and the mockery of the Philistines whom he had so often reduced to dust in the prime of his strength—no, it is a thousand times better that we bear him, the day after tomorrow, to the grave where his wife lies at rest."[10]

The bereft friend wrote to Liebknecht on the day of death: "Despite the fact that I saw him this evening stretched out on his bed with the mask of death on his face, I just cannot think that this genial head has stopped impregnating the proletarian movement in both worlds with powerful thoughts. What we all are, we are through him, and what the movement is today, it is through his theoretical and practical activity; without him, we would still be in a confused mess."

And yet the effects which originated from his activity were at that time still in the beginning stages; in Germany the exceptional law against the socialists was repressing, everywhere the insight into the inner necessity of the socialistic endeavor was still weak; the learned world, especially, was indifferent or simply rejecting. Today, one can hardly open a book, a pamphlet, a magazine, or a newspaper dealing with economic and social questions, without encountering Marx or Marxist theories being debated, lauded, or refuted. His work has become his monument. Politics and literature are filled with his ideas. It cannot be foreseen how strongly and how long he will continue to be influential. Whether this influence is wholesome or harmful for folk and humanity is a different question, but his ideas have become world-moving.

Marx was a man of medium height; seated, however, he appeared somewhat taller, broad shouldered, and of upright carriage. His head was round, surrounded by a mighty growth of hair and beard, which in his young years was shining black, became gray early, and then was snow-white; his forehead was beautifully rounded; his dark eyes flamed vivaciously; his nose was small with broad flanks. The expression of his face was energy, clarity, and kindness. His Jewish nature was not noticeable in his appearance, at least not in the sense of the restless, often play-acting gesticulating Jew of low height, with a tripping gait, whose exterior is so obtrusive that one thinks of him (unjustly) as typical. Marx was a simple man. He loved simplicity. His distaste for Lassalle and other Jews was perhaps so great because he always kept in mind his own descent. Marx was a true intellectual and in many respects a genuine German intellectual. He lived in and with books. He devised the greatest plans, drew up the keenest sketches, collected and studied, wrote and erased, and was too diverse, too polyphonous by nature to finish what he wanted to do. To be sure, the exterior limitations to his economic situation and to his health were powerful. But "a real strong heart cannot be killed." The elastic nature that he possessed was able to bring back the cheerfulness and the courage which he needed for his immense activity; although his excessive work, especially at night, again and again reminded him of his mortality.

Marx was a philosopher. He never denied the young-Hegelian in him, although he learned, contrary to Hegel, to think "materialistically"—or one could better say "realistically." The study of the philosophy of law linked to his first field of study, his studies of the social question and the great pains he took to understand the history of the development of economic theories, had at quite an early date enlarged and deepened his intellect. But his thoughts continued to roam into new domains, either through daily events or through new books, and through many stimulations from Engels. The daily events took all the more of his time, since he had to make his living from them. In the time of his most industrious labor, the new book by Darwin, called the *Origin of the Species,* came to him from a field which was otherwise foreign to him; he read some other literature of this kind, but was little furthered thereby. The diversity of his intellectual life is witnessed, among other things, by his idea mentioned above of writing an outline of the Hegelian logic, through which the core of the dialectic was to be made generally understood. Furthermore, he carried the plan of a history of philosophy, and even in his later days he studied mathematics so industriously that he developed his own theory of differential calculus. Therefore, one must often think with regret that he was not able to concentrate sufficiently. But it was a part of his being that he was not only a thinker and theoretician, but also a revolutionary politician and wanted to be one. His indignation and hate for capitalism, his decisive partiality for the working classes was the source of his power and the counterbalance of his fate. He thought, of course, that as a thinker he could fulfill his destiny in its fullest meaning and it was his highest ambition to provide the socialistic endeavors with a foundation based on a scientific and thoroughly grounded theory. Despite his many significant accomplishments, his life leaves one with the impression of tragedy. Especially tragic is the fact that he had during his lifetime, but even more so in his later transfiguration as a hero, become a decisive authority and, therefore, an oracle. As such, he came to be interrogated in vain, because the ambiguity of his answers inflame the passions of his followers against each other.

Marx was a person of the most noble disposition of intellect and sentiment. Originally passionate and impetuous, he mastered his moods in his later years and generally rendered judgment with a superior consciousness. Parts from the speech about the civil war in France are relapses into the pathos of his youth, which can be explained by the immense impression the Commune made on him. Moreover, his revolutionary sentiment became transfigured through his belief in the better future of humanity. As much as he denied all conclusions from sentiment, he himself still felt deeply the pains of the workers, and he took a vital interest in the bettering of their conditions. This stamp is also manifest in his work and, therefore, it has engraved itself so deeply into the souls of the working class in Germany, in Europe, and even on the other continents.

NOTES AND REFERENCE

1. T.N.: S W I 490.
2. T.N.: M E S C 295.
3. T.N.: Ibid., p. 296.
4. T.N.: Ibid.
5. T.N.: Ibid., p. 298.
6. T.N.: S W I 488.
7. T.N.: Ibid., p. 489.
8. T.N.: Ibid., p. 495.
9. T.N.: Ibid., p. 539.
10. T.N.: M E S C 435–36.

PART II

His Teachings

Chapter 1

CRITIQUE OF THE POLITICAL

ECONOMY—

THE THEORY OF VALUE

The quintessence of Marx's theory and his teachings is to be found in his criticism of political economics. "The" political economy (or national economics, an expression Marx does not use) is that form of thought which we today identify as "classical" political economics. Marx strongly differentiated this brand of economics from what he called the "vulgar" economics. The first was for him a rigorous science; the latter, a popularized shallow version of the principles of political economics. As is well known, the major principles were developed primarily in England, their greatest exponents and creators being Adam Smith and David Ricardo, Smith's predecessors, the physiocrats in France. The founder, William Petty, was, however, for Marx another Englishman. At the height of its development, classical national economics maintained the practical generalized principle that the commonweal is served best through internal and external free trade. Following this thinking, internal free trade, i.e., free competition, is most important for the distribution of the "gross national product." According to this general idea just distribution of production takes place so that the three great income classes are formed according to their contribution to production, in that ground rent falls to property, profits to capital, and wages to labor. In this presentation, capital always engenders production, and pays landed property and labor for their use the share which they earn. According to what rules can they insist on their share, and what share remains for capital? These are the first problems arising from this conceptualization.

It is assumed as natural and necessary that in the division of labor each producer makes that commodity which is best suited to his situation and facilities and in competition with others who in turn act likewise. All produce for the market, for an exchange; that is, for the most general medium of exchange —money. According to what rules does this exchange into money occur? This is the third main problem and the most central one, because on it is based the distribution of money income. The theory is this: There are various fluctuating prices, the market prices, but there is also a natural price, that price which corresponds to the value of the commodity: this value is the exchange value, to be strictly differentiated from the use value. The exchange value is that value which simply, as in the case of a sum of money, can purchase or in a sense be turned into desired goods selected at random from a great variety of products. Only in exchange, that is, as commodity is compared with commodity and therefore also compared with money which represents all commodities, is the value brought to light. Therefore, the third problem is that of value.

The customary conception, which was also represented by Adam Smith, is to see value as composed of the various kinds of income. Yet Adam Smith also adhered to a contrary, and more fundamental, point of view which sees value as prior to the kinds of income which are seen as emerging later, said value being incorporated in these forms of income. Ricardo develops this viewpoint further, saying that with the exception of those goods which cannot be increased through human effort, the exchange value of all goods is determined by the amount of labor which has been put into their production. Marx, who wrote broadly about the development of the theories of value, gave profound special attention to the development and dissolution of Ricardo's school and takes this as a starting point for his criticism of political economy. He borrows from Ricardo that fundamental theoretical position, which he characterizes by saying that the value of a commodity is determined by the labor in it. That is, the work time —or as he liked to say figuratively "congealed labor time," which is the time socially necessary to produce a commodity at a given stage of production—is that labor required to produce and deliver a commodity to the market. This labor, said Marx, constitutes its value. His new and critical conclusions, as

Marx sees them, are these: (1) labor itself has a dual character depending on whether it is expressed in use value or exchange value. (2) Before any differentiation of the types of income is made, a differentiation must be made of the value of the labor power that is contained in each product as produced by labor itself, and the surplus value *("Mehrwert")*, which will be treated independently of its special forms of profit, interest, property rent, etc., because these latter are still not distinguishable elements of the general form of the surplus value. (3) For the first time labor wages are presented as a hidden relationship, composed of hourly rates and piece rates.

Marx stressed repeatedly that this is the best part of his book (Vol. 1 of *Das Kapital*) or that these are the book's three totally new elements. In this first volume he developed the process by which capital is produced. He showed how a commodity, as the elementary form of wealth of modern society, receives its form of value through exchange: the simple form of value changes into a developed form, the latter changes into the general form of value, and out of this arises money. The theory puts highest priority on identifying the puzzling character of the product of labor when it changes into the form of a commodity and is derived out of this very form. Value is a hidden relationship between persons; consumer goods as value are portrayed as a social product like language. Social relationships are treated here as independently pursued private endeavors which form the complex of the social labor, and are direct social relationships of persons to one another. However, these appear as "objective" relationships of persons, and as social relationships of things. Here labor produces use value; there, if labor is viewed quantitatively only, differentiation presupposes its qualitative unity or equality; that is, its reduction to abstract human labor. From this exchange process springs the circulation of goods based on money, which in its form as a measure of value is the immanent measure of the value of goods, of labor time.

A special section deals with the transformation of money into capital. Money as money and money as capital is first of all only differentiated through its form of circulation: the only end of simple circulation of commodities is the exclusive acquisition of use values, but the circulation of money as capital is its own end, for only within this constantly renewing movement is value increased through constant growth: the movement of capital is therefore boundless.

The exchange of goods in its pure form is an exchange of equivalents. The accumulation of surplus value and thus the transformation of money into capital can neither be explained by noting that the seller may sell goods above their value, nor by noting that the buyer may buy them below their value. Surplus value cannot result from circulation except when there is a commodity which is itself the source of value; and there is only one such special commodity: labor power. It is the only source of surplus value, and becomes this as soon as its productive power has become large enough to produce, through labor, more value than is incorporated in labor power itself. It is theoretically assumed that the value of the commodity, labor power, is determined in the same manner as that of all other commodities, through the amount of social labor time necessary for its reproduction; that is, through the labor time contained in foodstuffs and other utilities which the worker needs for himself and his children according to his historically and morally conditioned customs and standard of living. The value of labor power includes in addition the costs of education and training in various occupations.

The buyer of labor power acquires the use value of labor for a determined time; e.g., the working day of twelve hours. Because social labor as such has a dual character—it produces (1) (particular) use value, e.g., a piece of cloth; (2) (general) value—it again produces within a certain given time the value of the labor power from which it originates. If the working time is longer than this given time, then the extra time results in surplus value. It is indeed a very plain arithmetic calculation.

Marx puts great emphasis on the fact that in his theory, labor wages are not the price of labor, but of labor power. Labor as a value-generating principle has no value in itself. It cannot change into a commodity, but the capability of the worker and his willingness to work, if he is cognizant of them and offers them, can do so. Through this differentiation, Marx wanted to solve the difficult theoretical problems that never would have been solved by the Ricardo school: that labor, which forms the measure of value, according to Ricardo, is paid when it becomes value; so that the whole value of the produce would have to be incorporated in the wages of labor. For Marx, however, it is necessary to derive the other forms of income from labor wages, which are seen by him as parts of the surplus value. The production of surplus value is characteristic of the capitalistic mode of production. It is a historical phenomenon, the origin, development, and decline of which must be made known; that is, it must be deduced from its essence which is characterized by the fact that, (1) it is the production of goods: it makes production of goods a principle of social production by generalizing it; but that it is (2) essentially the production of surplus value.

Marx distinguished between absolute surplus value and relative surplus value. Absolute surplus value originates in the lengthening of the labor day beyond the point in which the worker reproduces the value of his labor power by the acquisition of this extra labor by the buyer, i.e., the owner of labor power. This constitutes the general foundation of the capitalistic system. However, there is a special method of increasing surplus labor through lessening of the necessary labor. Thus with the length of the working day remaining the same, the less working time required to produce an equivalent product measured in amount of wages, the more surplus labor there is, which generates more surplus value. This is what capital is interested in—the surplus labor which creates surplus value. We are dealing here with production of the *relative* surplus value: relative surplus value has a revolutionary effect on the technical processes of labor and on social groupings. As for the other form—the production of absolute surplus value—the formal subordination of labor under capital, as in cottage industries or in the usury practiced on artisans, etc., is sufficient for its creation. This is the foundation on which the specific capitalistic manner of production grows and in which labor really knuckles under to the power of capital.

Capitalistic production as a specific mode of production is firstly and mainly a means whereby *relative* surplus value is

produced. As such it has a decisive influence on those branches
of industry whose products determine the value of labor
power; that is, it belongs either to the category of generally
used foodstuffs or to goods which can take their place and
stretches from there to include also the means of production
for the fabrication of such goods. In general, competition in-
duces capital to manufacture goods more cheaply. The common aim of the competitors is to minimize the value of labor
power in relation to the value of the whole product. Therefore,
despite keeping the length of the work day the same, surplus
value is increased. The general procedure for making goods
cheaper is the increase of the productive power of labor: surplus value grows in a one-to-one relationship in the development of the productive power of labor.

The special methods of producing surplus value can be
broadly outlined as follows: (1) *Cooperation,* i.e., the planned
teamwork of many involved in the same process of production
or in different but interlinked processes. The worker is
stripped of his individuality but develops his species-conscious-
ness. The separated individual work processes are converted
into a combined social process. The commands of capital become a condition for production as indispensable in production as the command of the general on the battle field. This
management of capital has a dual content because the process
of production is, on the one hand, social process; on the other
hand, it is a process whereby capital is made use of and as such
is determined by the antagonism between exploiter and the
exploited. the form is despotical, direct supervision which in a
way becomes a form of wage labor. When placed under the
conditions of cooperation, the social productive power develops itself gratuitously for capital; it appears as the immanent
productive power of capital; cooperation itself appears as a
specific form of the capitalist productive process; its simple
form appears as a special form of the capitalistic mode of production beside its more developed forms.

As such then (2) is to be seen the division of labor and the
mode of *manufacturing* determined by it. The source of
manufacturing is dual: (a) Union of various, otherwise independent trades under the direction of capital for the joint manu-

facture of a product. The consequence is specialization of these trades for a more narrow sphere of action; and (b) The same craftsmen are brought into one shop and the work divided among them. In both cases the result is a production mechanism, whose parts are people, whose basis is a handicraft—the combined total worker is made up of former part-owners or artisans. The productive power of labor is increased in comparison to that of the independent artisans; this is brought about by technical skill of the worker and improvement of his tools.

"The organization of manufacture has two fundamental forms [determined by the nature of the article produced]. This article either results from the mere mechanical fitting together of partial products made independently, or owes its completed shape to a series of connected processes and manipulations."[1] The second type is the perfected form of manufacture. Here develops out of the combination of detail workers, the composite worker *(Gesamtarbeiter)*, one who masters the various stepwise processes; this is achieved by means of the same worker being bound to the same partial work operation, and by means of the provision that for each special function a given number of workers is fixed. Each group consists of homogeneous elements and forms a special organ of this composite worker, who at the same time represents the specific mechanism of the manufacturing process. Unskilled labor, which is excluded from the crafts and guilds is included now. This is a devaluation of labor power compared to that of the crafts and guilds, resulting in capital gains as well as an enhanced continuity, uniformity, regularity, order and intensity of labor.

The division of labor within society and the division of labor within manufacture are, despite many analogies and connections, essentially different. Indeed, in their development they stand to each other in a converse relationship. In the division of labor among society's units, independent manufacturers of goods compete with each other; in manufacture, despotical order and centralization reign. The anarchy of the societal division of labor is characteristic of the capitalistic mode of production, while in earlier phases of development planned and authoritarian organization existed. The division of labor for manufacturing mutilates the worker and stamps him as property of capital. As it progresses, the division of labor develops into a conscious, planned, and systematic form of the capitalistic mode of production. However, as such it is only a special method for developing new social productive powers of labor, and, through this, to produce relative surplus value or to augment the process whereby capital is invested at the expense of the workers. But manufacture is limited by its own narrow, technical basis, and especially in lack of discipline and subordination on the part of the workers. The "period of manufacture" remains a time of imperfect capitalistic production: the period Sombart called Early Capitalism.

It is only (3) through the machine by which capital can raise the productive power of labor and thereby the production of the relative surplus value to its highest. "The [machine] tool . . . *(Werkzeugmaschine)* is that part of the machinery with which the industrial revolution of the eighteenth century started. And to this day it constantly serves as such a starting point whenever a handicraft, or a manufacture, is turned into an industry carried on by machinery."[2] "The machine, which is the starting point of the industrial revolution, supersedes the workman who handles a single tool by a mechanism which operates a number of similar tools and which is set in motion by a single motive power, whatever the form of that power may be."[3] The machine tool is followed by the motor, which is freed from the limitations of human hand or foot power and can activate many work machines simultaneously. At the same time the mechanism of transmission, that is, the third part of all developed machinery evolves into a vast apparatus.

The actual complex machine system is to be differentiated from the cooperation of many similar machines. Here the division of labor is repeated as a combination of machines with specialized functions. In manufacture the subjective principle of the division of labor, which tailors the process to the worker, is still valid. In the complex machine system the total process is objectively dissolved into its constituent phases: the mechanism itself conveys the material from one phase of production into the next. "Here we have, in the place of the isolated machine, a mechanical monster whose body fills whole factories and whose demon power, at first veiled under the slow and measured motions of his giant limbs, at length breaks out into the fast and furious whirl of his countless working organs."[4] Big industry frees itself from its original foundations of craft and guild production and manufacture by seizing its characteristic means of production, the machine itself, in that it produces machines through machines—thereby lays for itself an adequate technical foundation. The worker now is confronted with the objective mechanism of production in the form of a ready material condition for production. The means of production have become so powerful that they can replace to a large extent human power by natural power, and routine experience by conscious use of natural science.

The machine creates no new value but it adds value to the product by attrition of its own value. In itself it possesses far larger value than the means of production of the handicrafts and manufacture. Therefore, the difference between its performance and that part of its value which it loses through wear and tear is much greater. Apart from average daily attrition and the use of auxiliary substances such as oil, coal, etc., the means of work are free like natural power; therefore, the extent of this gratuitous service is much larger with machines. The production of machines by machines, however, diminishes their value in proportion to its diffusion and effectiveness so that it also gives less value to the product, and thus becomes more productive and more equal in its service to that of natural power.

The production of machinery must always cost less labor than the labor it replaces. The capitalistic mode of production, however, always asks what the difference is between the price of the machine and the price of the labor power which is being replaced: the cheaper the price of labor power, the less the temptation to replace it with machines. The machine reacts on the worker, making the labor of women and children possible where formerly, adult male muscle power was necessary. Thus, with capital's expansion of the field of exploitation, the degree of exploitation is also expanded and the value of labor power is diminished. Hence, the contract between worker and capitalist changes forcibly (because the worker can now also dispose of the labor power of women and children).

Although the increase of relative surplus value through the means of increasing the productive power of labor is different from the increase of the absolute surplus value through lengthening of the working day, it should be noted that the machine is, notwithstanding, the most powerful means of increasing productivity of work and of effecting the lengthening of the working day—if only through the fact that the motion and activity of the means of production are now independent of the worker. Not only wear and tear, but also the idleness of the machine affects its value. Besides those material considerations, there is also a "moral" attrition—its value can decrease through diminishing of labor time which is necessary for its own reproduction, or for that required to produce a better machine. This entails a special incitement to lengthen the working day, because the total value of the machine is then reproduced more quickly. Furthermore, the expenditures necessary for the exploitation of the means of production decrease the longer the work day becomes, and this weighs more heavily the more capital is invested in machines. It must not remain unused for long periods, therefore, effort must be put forth to lengthen the work day. In the use of machines lies a contradiction insofar as the one factor, which conditions the volume of surplus value, becomes larger, namely, its rate, which is increased when the other factor, the number of workers, becomes smaller. This also drives capital to lengthen the work day, without being conscious of it. The machine displaces the worker, creates a surplus working population, and throws aside all moral and natural limits of the working day. In essence the machine is the most powerful means available for shortening the working day, but in the hands of capital it acts to the disadvantage of the worker and the workingman's family.

A legally limited worktime is society's reaction to this—the indignation of the working class forces the state to enact this into law. On the one hand, this leads to a quickened development in the system of industrial machines; on the other hand, to a compressing or intensification of work. Especially through the increased speed of the machine and the expanded arena of work of a laborer, his activity is increased, which in turn redounds to the production of relative surplus value. The traditional system of the division of labor within the shop is technically thrown overboard by the machine. But lifelong specialization of handling a tool changes in the *factory* into a lifelong specialization of operating a machine, and thus the worker must transform himself into a part of this machine. The general essence of the capitalistic mode of production "[makes it possible through] the factory system for this inversion, by which the working conditions use the laborer for the first time, to acquire technical and palpable reality."[5] This, and the composition of the labor force constituted of men, women, adults, adolescents, children, bring forth a barrack-like discipline, a militaristic structure of labor within the factory.

In all phases of development, labor fights capital. It fights the machine as the material means by which capital exists. The means of production compete with the worker. They eventually kill the worker. They become the most powerful weapon by which to beat down the increasing demands. Those workers displaced by the machine increase the number of workers available in the labor market, and some capital is made available to engage these workers. However, in the wake of machines, new branches of production and new fields of work are created through the industrial revolution. In those branches of industry which furnish the basic means of work to other branches expanded by machines, production is increased. This is especially true of machine production as well as those lines of production which further refine the industrial products. A famous example is cotton weaving based on machine spinning. Furthermore, the production of luxury goods grows together with surplus value, as well as unproductive use of a growing part of the proletariat. Despite the displacement of workers by the machine, by increasing the number of like factories, the total number of factory workers can exceed the number of artisans and manufacturing workers formerly employed in the same type of industry. A favorite sphere of production always attracts more massive amounts of capital. The expansion of large industry is only limited by raw materials and the market

demand. An *international division of labor* is created, which
reserves a part of the globe for agriculture to be supplied with
industrial products by factories which are expanding and
blindly competing with each other. Therefore, markets fluctu-
ate from oversupply and undersupply. Periods such as the
following develop: (a) medium activity, (b) rising demands, (c)
overproduction. These are followed by periods of (d) crises and
(e) recession. Thus, the level of living of the worker is made
increasingly insecure and unpredictable through the machine.

Large industry does away with the cooperation resting in
the handicrafts and division of labor. It reacts to early manufacture and cottage industry making cheap labor the rule. Manufacture is pressed toward the capitalistic economization of
work conditions, and cottage industry becomes a sphere of
exploitation established in the background of big industry.
Both are made gradually to go over to the factory system of
industry, especially when factory legislation is applied to the
earlier modes of production. "Factory legislation, that first
conscious and methodological reaction of society against the
spontaneously developed form of the process of production, is
[as we have seen], just as much the necessary product of modern industry as cotton yarn . . . spinning machines and the
electric telegraph."[6] The capitalistic mode of production inherently excludes all rational improvement beyond a certain
point. These legal actions are the first step made to blast the
shell of the capitalistic order which restricts the technical development of labor use. Hence, the demand for necessary
breathing space for each worker would attack the capitalist
mode of production at its roots. The factory system itself could
engender the education for the future, provided that it were
given an adequate social form. Thus, just as the contradiction
between the division of labor in early manufacturing and the
essence of modern mass industry has already forcefully come
to the fore, so also the social division of labor would finally be
dissolved, once the capitalistic form of production and its corresponding economic labor relationships were overcome.

The technical basis of modern mass industry is revolutionary. In it the functions of workers and the social combinations
of the work process are constantly overthrown and changed.

Through these changes the social division of labor is constantly revolutionized and volumes of capital and masses of laborers are thrown from one branch of production into another. On the one hand, change of work, all-round versatility of the laborer, is the demand of modern large industry, while, on the other hand, modern industry reproduces the ossified specialization in the division of labor. This absolute contradiction cancels all the peace, certainty, and security of the life conditions of the laborer. By taking from him the means of production, the system takes away a vital instrument of his and threatens to make him superfluous because of his detail labor functions. This endless sacrifice of the proletariat, measureless waste of work power, devastation through societal anarchy, is the nature of modern capitalistic enterprise.

Through its catastrophes, large industry makes it a matter of life and death to accept, as a general social law of production, mobility in work arrangements, versatility of the worker, and to tailor circumstances as to bring this law to its normal realization—to train humans to be equally competent for varying demands of work, to replace the detailed worker by the developed well-rounded total individual for whom various social functions are his alternating modes of activity. Elements in this revolution have already spontaneously developed in the form of polytechnical and agronomical schools. The successful conquest of political power by the working class will also lead to the introduction of theoretical and practical technology in the working class schools.

The capitalistic mode of production and its corresponding economic working conditions are diametrically opposed to such revolutionary ferments. Large industry liquidated the economic base of the family, its corresponding family labor, and the old family relationships. The capitalistic form of the family brought parental authority into misuse. However, it has found, simultaneously, with the roles into which adolescents and children are brought into the socially organized process of production away from the sphere of the household, a new economic basis for a higher form of family and relationship between the sexes. The factory legislation is also in this respect preparation; the necessity to generalize it into a law of all social production arises out of the historical development of large industry itself. Although this legislation, as physical and intellectual means of protection for the working class, becomes inevitable, it accelerates the basic process of development; that is, the concentration of capital and the sole dominance of the factory regimen. With capital becoming the generalized universal form dominating everything, the direct struggle against this domination also becomes a general feature of society. Together with the material conditions and the social combination of the production process, the contractions and antagonism of its capitalistic form reach a stage of maturation while, at the same time, laying the building stones for a new society and for the revolution of the old society.

The industrial revolution asserts itself also in *agriculture*, especially through increasing unemployment. It annihilates the bulwark of the old society, the peasant, and substitutes for him the wage laborer. It tears asunder the original old family bond of union between agriculture and manufacture which held together the undeveloped forms of both, while at the same time it produces the material conditions for a new higher synthesis of both. By disturbing the man-land relationship through the accumulation of the population in large centers, it destroys at the same time the physical health of the laborer in the town, and the intellectual and spiritual life of the laborer in the country. But this development also makes it necessary to restore this man-land relationship systematically as a ruling law of social production, in a manner adequate to full human development. The capitalistic form of large industry develops the technique and combination of the social production process while concurrently undermining the sources of wealth—the soil and the worker.

The natural productive powers of labor and the historically developed social productive powers both appear as productive powers of capital into which they are incorporated. The process of production remains a relationship between man and nature for the well-rounded total worker; thus, the concept of productive work has enlarged its meaning, but it becomes narrow and restricted insofar as surplus value becomes the decisive mark of the productive worker. Surplus value is given by nature, in the sense that each degree of increased productivity of work beyond that amount which is necessary to maintain the worker and his race through provision of foodstuffs is surplus value, making it possible for others to accumulate surplus value. But the appropriation of surplus value becomes systematic in capitalistic production and is increased to such an extent that the difference between absolute and relative surplus value becomes noticeable.

The extensive magnitude of labor, the length of the work day (A), its intensive magnitude (B), and the productivity of labor (C) together determine the relative amounts of cost and surplus value. These change according to whether (1) A and B are given, C variable; (2) A and C are given, B variable; (3) B and C are given, A variable; (4) A, B, C are variable simultaneously, which again allows for many combinations: the most important developmental tendency is characterized by increases in B and C with simultaneous decreases in A. For instance, in the case of an overthrow of the capitalistic mode of production, A would be limited to necessary labor. Labor itself, however, would increase in intensity, because: (1) the life conditions and standard of workers would increase and (2) a part of the present excess labor would be included, namely, labor now necessary for the social reserves and accumulation funds. "The more the productiveness of labor increases, the more the working day can be shortened; and the more the working day is shortened, the more the intensity of labor can increase." From a social viewpoint, the productiveness of labor increases in the same ratio as the economy of labor which, in its turn, includes not only economy of the means of production but also the avoidance of all useless labor. The capitalist mode of production while, on the one hand, enforcing economy in each individual business, on the other hand, begets, by its anarchical system of competition, the most outrageous squandering of labor power and of the social means of production, not to mention the creation of a vast number of employments at present indispensable, but in themselves superfluous."[7] Furthermore, when B and C are given, that part of the social labor (i.e., the work day) which is necessary for the material production must also be differentiated from that part which becomes available for the intellectual and social recreation of the individual. This part becomes larger the more equally work is shared among all those members of society able to work. In capitalistic production the worker is separated from the product. In fact, this is a specific characteristic of the capitalistic relationship although apparently there is an associational relationship in which capital and labor divide the product according to its various constituent factors. "Capital . . . is essentially the command over unpaid labor . . . surplus value . . . is in substance the materialization of unpaid labor."[8]

Labor wage is not the price of labor, but of labor *power.* Labor has no value; it is the substance and immanent measure of values, but labor power whose function is labor has value. The form of wages for labor which appears to be the payment for labor itself is all the more significant because the money relationship it conceals hides the unpaid labor of the wage laborer. This happens in the same way that property relationships hide the fact that the slave is performing work. It is significant because all legal conceptions of those involved rest on the illusion that all labor is paid for. All mystifications of the capitalist mode of production arise from this. Of the two elementary forms of labor wages, time wage and piece wage, the latter is a transformation of the first. Piece wages facilitate the subletting of work which ends in sweatshop labor and the related contracts with foremen who undertake the hiring and remuneration of auxiliary workers. This form, corresponding best to the capitalistic mode of production, becomes a general rule under the factory laws, because under this form capital can only intensify the labor day. Changes of piece wages breed struggles between capital and labor, especially when these changes result from the increased productive power of labor, because the worker does not know that even the piece rate is only the expression in price of a determined work time; hence, he objects to the consequences which capital draws therefrom.

The process of production must continue in every societal form. It is always at the same time a process of reproduction. If production is capitalistic, then reproduction is too; it is then only a means to reproduce the advanced value as capital. The process produces and reproduces the capitalistic relationship, on the one side the capitalist, on the other the wage laborer. The worker continuously produces the objective wealth as capital: a power which is alien to him and exploits and dominates him. The mere continuity of the production process or the simple reproduction transforms sooner or later any necessary capital into accumulated capital or capitalized surplus value. Capital continuously produces a labor power as a subjective source of wealth, separated from its objective means of realization, abstractly existing in the mere embodiment of the laborer. From a social point of view, the working class is equally an appendage of capital and the work instruments, even outside the direct work process. Indeed, in the same way as traditions and the accumulation of skills are included in the reproduction of the working class from one generation to the next, so the capitalist too, must count the presence of a skilled working class among his conditions of production. Reproduction or accumulation grows beyond simple reproduction, in that parts of the unused surplus value bring new surplus value as additional capital. All capital originally advanced becomes minimal in the flux of production when compared to the surplus value or surplus product transformed back into capital. This divides itself, like the original capital, into constant capital (means of production) and variable capital (labor power). Accumulation for the sake of accumulation and therefore limitation of his own consumption funds, i.e., thrift, becomes a must for the capitalist because of the social mechanism in which he is only a driving gear, and because of competition which decrees that capital must be expanded if it is to be kept. However, on a higher stage of development a conventional degree of waste becomes a conspicuous display of wealth and therefore a means of credit, that is, not only a satisfaction of the pleasure drive, but also necessary for business: such luxury is incorporated into the representational costs of capital. Often even parts of necessary consumption funds for the worker are transformed into an accumulation fund of capital.

The degree of productivity of labor is another important factor in the accumulation of capital. Its increase allows the consumption by the capitalist to grow without decreasing his capital; sometimes even a relative increase in his accumulation of capital may take place. Labor's productivity can accelerate accumulation even when the supplemental capital decreases because the real wage never rises with the productivity of labor. It raises the value and mass of the means of production put into movement by the given amounts of labor. The dogma of national economics concerning the wage fund is based on the fact that the worker is passive when the capitalist differentiates or divides between his consumption and his accumulation funds, and on the fact that the worker can only in exceptional circumstances increase his wage at the expense of the capitalist.

A differentiation is to be made between the value composition of constant and variable capital, on the one hand, and between the technical composition of capital, means of production, and available labor power, on the other. Insofar as the first is determined by the latter, the first is called the organic composition of capital. If the latter remains constant, growth of capital includes growth of the component now transformed into labor power: rising demand for labor increases wages. Accumulation reproduces the capital relationship at a higher level in a stepwise expansion: more or larger capitalists at the one pole, more wage laborers at the other. At the same time the real wage can increase; that is, the unpaid labor can be diminished, but this decrease can never go so far as to threaten the system itself. Thus, there must continue a steady reproduction of the capital relationship at ever-rising levels, and it must always expand stepwise. Here the law holds that the constant part of capital (the bulk of the means of production) grows in proportion to the variable part of capital (the bulk of labor power). However, the value of the mass of the means of production sinks in comparison to its size. A certain accumulation of capital, the "original" one, is the precondition for the specific capitalist mode of production. But the one also conditions the other and vice versa, and both contribute toward the continuous diminution of the variable part of capital. The accumulation and the concentration accompanying it are splintered in many ways, and the growth of functioning capitals is crisscrossed by the formation of new and the splitting of old capitals. "This splitting-up of the total social capital into many individual capitals or the repulsion of its fractions one from another, is counteracted by their attraction. . . . It is concentration of capitals . . . expropriation of capitalist by capitalist, transformation of many small into few large capitals. . . . This is centralization proper, as distinct from accumulation and concentration."[9] In the competitive fight of capitals, credit becomes a new and awesome weapon—finally a terrifying social mechanism for centralization of capitals. It acts mainly as associations of capitals (stocks); it increases and accelerates the effect of accumulation; at the same time it expands and hastens the revolution in the technical composition of capital. The masses of capital welded together in this manner reproduce and increase like the others, only faster, and thereby become new important levers for social accumulation. Labor demand decreases relative to the extent of the total capital and in accelerated progression with the growth of capital.

In relation to its energy and extent, the capitalistic accumulation always produces a relative surplus of the labor population, that is, relative for the average utilization needs of capital. With the accumulation of capital produced by themselves, the laborers thus increasingly produce the means to make themselves supernumerary—a population law characteristic of the capitalistic mode of production. This overpopulation in turn becomes a lever for capitalistic accumulation, even a condition for the existence of this mode of production. The characteristic life course of modern industry, with alternating expansion and contraction, rests in the steady formation, in the greater or lesser absorption and rebuilding of the "industrial reserve army." Contrary to economic dogma, the movement of capital in today's industry is not dependent on the absolute movement of the population masses; it is the other way around. The expansion and contraction of capital, its stronger or weaker strivings for utilization, regulate the demand and supply of work, and thereby the alternating relationship whereby the working class is split into an active army and a reserve army. A countereffect is possible when the trade unions try to organize a planned cooperation between the employed and unemployed. The relative overpopulation—apart from the great periodical forms of the industrial cycle—manifests itself in

three forms: fluid, latent, and stagnant. The first form is found
in the centers of big industry; the second, in the rural country-
side; and the third, is part of the active army; limited however,
to irregular employment usually found in the realm of the
cottage industries because this population perpetuates itself
through strong natural increase. The most depressing conditions due to the relative overpopulation is the sphere of pauperism which besides the "Lumpenproletariat," consists of: (1)
employable persons, (2) orphans and children of paupers, (3)
unemployable persons—victims of industry, cripples, the sick,
aged, widows, etc. With social wealth and functioning capital
grows the industrial reserve army. The larger it is in relationship to the active army, the more massive is the consolidated
overpopulation, the "Lazarus layer" of the proletariat—the
larger both of them are, the larger is official pauperism.

This is the absolute general law of capitalistic accumulation
which, in reality, nevertheless, is modified by various circumstances. This law chains the laborer more tightly to capital than
the wedges of Hephaestus chained Prometheus to the rocks.
The accumulation of wealth at the one pole is matched by
accumulation of misery, work, agony, and moral degradation
at the opposite one, revealing the antagonistic character of
capitalistic accumulation, hence, of the capitalistic property
relationships on the whole. This characteristic becomes obvious in the miserable living conditions in the big cities, and in
the living conditions of the itinerant worker, the truck-system
in the houses in the mining districts. Even the best paid part
of the working class is terribly affected by economic crises. The
development in England from 1846–1866 offers classical examples for all these phenomena. Nowhere is this antagonistic
character more brutally obvious than in the progress of English agriculture and in the regress of the English agricultural
worker with his miserable living accommodations, which
break down his resistance and make him slave of the landlord
and tenant farmers. The land, despite its steady relative overpopulation, is actually underpopulated as soon as as in intensive agriculture extra hands are required for farming. Exploitation of women and children and the "gang boss system" are
the consequences. The fate of Ireland offers a special illustra-
tion of the agricultural and industrial revolution.

As stated, the original accumulation was a precondition for this whole sequence of development. It was the historical process whereby the worker was separated from the means of production. The dissolution of the economic structure of feudal society had freed the elements of capitalistic society. This involved the displacement of the feudal lords who possessed the sources of wealth, and of the guild masters by the industrial capitalists. Also, this process was based on the separation of the farmer and small landowner from his soil and land. The abolition of serfdom was followed by dissolution of the feudal vassalage. It was the young feudal lords especially who drove out the peasants and usurped their land. Then came the Reformation and the confiscation of church property, later on the usurpation of and transformation into private property of land to which the lords held only feudal title or clan title, and finally the great theft of state domains, followed by the enclosure laws by which communal lands were usurped creating capitalistic tenant farms. Finally came clearing of the peasant farms of residents, transformation of cultivated fields into pastures, of sheep pastures into hunting-grounds, and expulsion and destruction of the independent yeomen. These were the methods used by the original accumulation, whereby the ground was prepared for capitalistic agriculture and the necessary supply of footloose proletariat was created for industry. The forcibly disowned farm population was whipped by terroristic laws into the discipline necessary for the system of wage labor. The rising bourgeoisie needed and used the power of the state to regulate the wages of labor through laws against high wages, against the coalition of workers so as to keep the workers in the normal degree of dependence. The capitalistic leaseholder developed through the age-old process of agricultural revolution. The thinning out of the independent land population matched the crowding of the industrial proletariat. The workers were set free, their means of livelihood and their labor material also become freely available, and the interior market was created. The rural cottage industry was destroyed, the divorce between agriculture and industry was completed through the dominance of big industry.

The various moments of original accumulation appear concentrated in the colonial system, in the state debt system—one of the most powerful levers of original accumulation—in the modern tax system, in the protectionist system. The colonial system, brutal power, and all methods use the power of the state to shorten the transitional period. "Force is the midwife of every old society pregnant with a new one. It, itself, is an economic power."[10] The transformation of the money capital, gained through usury and trade, into industrial capital, at first found its free playing field in harbor cities, guild-free villages, and other places in the country.

The original accumulation means, if not immediate transformation of serfs into free workers, the dissolution of private property based on one's own work. With the increasing misery also grows the indignation of the ever-swelling proletariat, schooled, unified, and organized through the mechanism of the capitalistic production process itself. "The monopoly of capital becomes a fetter upon the mode of production, which has sprung up and flourished along with, and under it. Centralization of the means of production and socialization of labor at last reach a point where they become incompatible with their capitalist integument. This integument is burst asunder. The knell of capitalist private property sounds. The expropriators are expropriated."[11]

The development of capitalism in colonies deserves special consideration. At first the wage laborer is missing there, the owner and master of his own labor conditions enriches himself rather than the capitalist through his labor. There, the separation of agriculture from industry has not yet taken place, nor has the destruction of the rural cottage industry. From whence then should come the interior market for capital? Each long-term undertaking which stretches over years and needs advances of fixed capital meets obstacles. The task is to make the supply of labor constant and regular, to increase the price of land so much that it (according to Wakefield) prevents the workers from becoming independent farmers until others arrive to take their place in the labor market—the so-called systematic colonization. In the United States this recipe became more and more superfluous through the natural development. But even capitalistic private property causes the destruction of private property built on one's own labor.

NOTES AND REFERENCES

1. T.N.: *Capital*, translated from the fourth German edition by E. Utermann (New York: The Modern Library, Random House, 1906) vol. 1, p. 375.
2. T.N.: Ibid., p. 407.
3. T.N.: Ibid., p. 410.
4. T.N.: Ibid., p. 417.
5. T.N.: Ibid., p. 462.
6. T.N.: Ibid., p. 526.
7. T.N.: Ibid., p. 581.
8. T.N.: Ibid., p. 585.
9. T.N.: Ibid., p. 686.
10. T.N.: Ibid., p. 824.
11. T.N.: Ibid., p. 837.

Chapter 2

THE RIDDLE OF THE AVERAGE
RATE OF PROFIT

Up to this point, we have separated the essence of Marx's theory and teachings from the first volume of *Das Kapital* (739 pages). Engels did justice to Marx's extensive preparations for the second and third volumes by putting together the splintered pieces of handwriting which were found in his estate of "papers left behind." The work, which in terms of its inner contents was fairly well rounded out and was to be the fourth volume dealing with the history of the theory, was edited as *Theorien über den Mehrwert (Theories About Surplus Value)* in 3 volumes (Stuttgart, 1910) by Kautsky, who changed the outer form.

The second volume, which deals with the circulation process was meant to complement the first volume, whose subject was the production process of capital. What is said in the first part ("The Metamorphosis of Capital or Its Circulation"), about the differences among money-capital, production-capital, and commodity-capital, and about turnover time and circulation costs, is important. Also worthwhile is the second part—the period required for the turnover of capital in general, working period, production time, circulation time, the effect of the turnover time on the magnitude of the capital advance, the turnover of variable capital, and the circulation of the surplus value. In the third part of the second volume some subjects treated in the first volume, such as reproduction and circulation of the social total capital, are further elaborated. The third, a quite extensive volume split into two parts, is meant to portray the "total process" of capitalistic production. Here the solution to the "riddle of the average rate of profit" is presented. This was Engels' description of the difficulties which arose from the contrast between the theory of value and actual experience. It seems to follow from the theory of value, according to which surplus value originates exclusively from the variable capital that is, the capital invested in labor wages, that the surplus value should be proportionately larger, the larger this variable part of capital is in relation to the constant part, and vice versa. But experience shows that profit is independent of this relationship, that it is a definite rate of the whole advanced capital, the height of which rate is stipulated by other momenta—it is this which Marx inexactly characterized as "average equality" *(durchschnittliche Gleichheit).* This "profit rate" is determined by two main factors: the rate of surplus value and the value composition of the capital; furthermore, it is affected by the turnover time, the price fluctuations of the raw materials, etc. The profit rate always expresses the surplus value rate lower than it is; even an increasing rate of surplus value has the tendency to be expressed in a falling profit rate. Both would be equal if capital were invested exclusively in labor wages (i.e., as if it were variable capital). When the goods are sold at their value, and value and price are the same, then in various spheres of production the rate of profit must be different. The whole system of capitalistic production would thereby be nullified.

In reality, it is *competition* which always affects the equalization of profits and forms a general profit rate in that the values of goods are transformed into *production prices,* otherwise called natural or necessary prices. The general profit rate, in that it rests in the equalization of various profit rates of various spheres, is also codetermined by the distribution of the total social capital in these various spheres. For capital, one part of the produced value exists in its "cost price," "the price of any commodity which is equal to its cost price plus that share of average profit on the total capital invested (not merely consumed) . . . is called its price of production."[1] The general profit rate is a meaningless and unscientific idea if the diversity of the profit rates is not developed from the value of the goods which are embodied in the surplus value. The various capitalists can be thought of as shareholders who share the whole profit according to the amount of capital invested in the undertaking by each, or according to the number of their shares. Goods are not exchanged merely as goods, but as *products of capitals,* which claim a share of the whole surplus value corresponding to their size; if they are equal in size, then they claim an equal share.

Production prices are a phenomenon which calls for a certain level of capitalistic development. The value of goods or the identity of the prices therewith, not only precede production prices theoretically but also historically; moreover, the law of value always dominates the movement of prices. Market value set by competition and individual value are different, even when value and price are generally equal; if the individual value is lower than the market value, there is an excess profit, while in the opposite case the whole surplus value would not be apparent. When demand is strong, the market value and thus the production price is set according to the goods produced under the worst conditions; when demand is weak, market value depends on the goods produced under the best conditions. There is no necessary, only a fortuitous, connection between that part of its total labor power which society uses for the production of a commodity, and the extent to which society demands satisfaction of a need which a given article is to fulfill. If excess supplies are manufactured, then a part of social labor time is wasted.

The exchange of goods in proportion to their values is in every case the natural—rational—law of their equilibrium; this is the point from which to start to explain deviations. During a certain period of time supply and demand match each other as average of past movements and as constant movements of their interaction *(ihres Widerspruchs).* Normally, market value (and market price), on the one hand, and demand and supply, on the other, determine each other; the relationship of these two is, therefore, not enough to explain the market value. In a straight exchange—be it goods against goods, or goods against money—each owner of goods (firstly, the producer) seeks at least to extract the same value he has thrown into the market. But in the capitalistic production, capital wants to extract the same *surplus value* as every other equally big capital and must therefore achieve prices which give average profit, that is, so-called production prices. Capital here becomes conscious of its social power, with each capitalist sharing it according to his share of the total capital of society. Compensation through competition happens more quickly, (1) the more mobile capital is and (2) the faster labor power can be moved from one sphere into another, from one place to another. Competition makes for false conceptions. But outside of competition there are reasons why certain capitalists ask for and receive compensation. Those reasons for compensation level out the participation in the total surplus value.

However, the steady, gradual growth of the constant part of capital, in relation to the variable part of capital or the increasingly higher organic composition of total capital, must under conditions in which there is an invariable rate of the surplus value cause a stepwise fall of the general profit rate, while at the same time the absolute volume of the profit increases. This is a law of great importance for capitalistic production, like the corresponding law, that the amount of the total capital is growing in a faster progression than the profit rate is falling therein. "Since everything appears inverted under competition, the individual capitalist may imagine . . . that he is reducing his profit on the individual commodity by cutting its price, but still making a greater profit on account of the larger quantity of commodities which he is selling."[2] Another expression of the law is found in the fact of falling commodity prices and the rise of the mass of big profits on the growing mass of cheaper goods.

The law itself only indicates a tendency; there are counteracting causes, opposing influences which can cancel out its effect and negate it; namely, "(1) raising the intensity of exploitation of labor, (2) depression of wages below their value, (3) cheapening of the elements of constant capital, (4) relative overpopulation, (5) foreign trade, which at first is a basis of the capitalist mode of production then becomes a product of the capitalist mode of production, through hastening the accumulation and otherwise raising the rate of profit, (6) increase in the sale and purchase of stocks the profit or return for which is hidden in interest and thus does not enter into equalization of the general rate of profit."[3]

The capitalist mode of production in the development of the productive powers thus encounters a barrier which has nothing to do with the production of wealth as such. If capital is adequate the direct production process—i.e., the generation of surplus value—finds no other barrier than the labor population, and when the labor population is given, the degree of exploitation is the crucial limiting factor. The second act of this process is in the market, the *realization* of the surplus value. Here the disproportionateness of the diverse spheres of production and the power of consumption brings about restraints; this power of consumption is curbed through the antagonism of the conditions of distribution. Expansion of the market is therefore made mandatory. But its connections and their conditions become more and more uncontrollable; the development of the productive power comes more and more into conflict with the restrictions of the market. The accumulation and the predominance of the constant capital becomes more decisively important and a larger part of the yearly product is now appropriated as replacement of used capital. The voluminousness of capital brings about centralization, i.e., decapitalization of smaller capitalists.

These same causes contribute to the fall of the profit rate as well as to the retardation of this fall. The general contradiction between expansion, on the one hand, and utilization of production, on the other, shows up in that the periodic devaluation of capital adversely affects the relationships of the circulation and reproduction processes of capital. The same is true of the formation of new capital whereby the fall of the rate of profit is halted. These adverse effects cause *crises* to arise as temporary violent solutions of the existing contradictions. The real barrier to capitalist production is *capital* itself. The unconditional development of the social productive powers constantly comes into conflict with the utilization of the existing capital, because utilization is the only and limited goal its masters have for it. With the fall of the rate of profit, which makes production profitable only for larger capitals, the smaller splintered capitals are driven into fraudulent uses. Overaccumulation of capital at a certain level leads to the idleness and even the destruction of capital, partly through nonutilization of the means of production and partly through other capital values. The stagnation causes wage decreases. Then the circumstances change for the better, and the cycle may be repeated. The same circumstances bring about overproduction of capital, of goods, and of workmen. All this overproduction is only relative, but such is the capitalistic mode of production. The absolute development of the productive powers is constantly getting into conflict with the specific conditions of production of capital. This is especially evident in that new branches of capital are no longer sufficiently profitable. If this ["absolute development of production"] came about, the vital spark or life of production would expire, for the profit rate is the driving force in capitalistic production.

NOTES AND REFERENCES

T.N.: In the short space alloted to the complicated problem of this chapter, Tönnies closely follows Marx as edited by Engels in the third volume of *Capital*, but the "riddle" should have the attention of economists. The senior translator, in his effort to locate in English the three passages cited below which follow Marx closely, found the following very helpful: Robert Freedman, ed., *Marx on Economics* (New York: Harcourt Brace, 1961). Short substantive treatments to be recommended here are the following: Gautam Mathur, "Marxist Economics in Relation to the Theory of Economic Growth and World Political Conditions," in Charles P. Loomis and Joan Rytina, *Marxist Theory and Indian Communism* (East Lansing, Mich.: Michigan State University Press, 1970) and Joan Robinson, *An Essay on Marxian Economics* (London: Macmillan & Co., 1942).

1. T.N.: Karl Marx, *Capital: A Critique of Political Economy*, vol. III (Chicago: Charles H. Kerr and Co., 1909) p. 181 after Freedman, op. cit., p. 153.

2. T.N.: Ibid. Marx, p. 271, and Freedman, p. 135.

3. T.N.: Ibid. Marx, pp. 271–81. Section headings are listed.

Chapter 3

THE CAPITALIST METHOD OF PRODUCTION AND ITS DEVELOPMENT

In the theory and teachings here presented, the *Critique of the Political Economy*, which Marx made his life's work, is encompassed in its main features. The subject of the third book was to be the division of surplus value into various independent forms as general profit, interest, merchants' profit, entrepreneural returns, ground rent. The expositions about the general rate of profit do, strictly speaking, not belong with this discussion because profit here is seen as the surplus value itself, insofar as it is calculated on the total capital. The other developments, especially those about merchants' profit and interest will later be discussed in detail in some other context. They do not belong to the most important characteristics of the theory.

What does it mean that the theory will be the critique of the political economy? In the following points the character of this critique is presented:

1. The classical adherents of this theory see the separation of capital and labor (as well as separation of land from both) as eternal and necessary, or, as in the case of Adam Smith, as given by the culture. Therefore, all progress in the direction of this separation is seen as progress of the culture. The criticism formulates the concept of the capitalistic mode of production: to have interpreted it and to have described its typical traits is, in truth, Karl Marx's great achievement. He characterized the capitalistic mode of production as the result of definite historical causes, having arisen in opposition to and in struggle against an earlier mode of production, which he customarily called the feudal. In his own purely economical (not political) analysis, this mode of production is characterized by the independent peasant farmer and artisan classes. Marx was not the

first person to recognize that he was here confronted with a development nor did he adequately describe this development, which was undoubtedly due to the fact it had at that time by no means reached its final stage. He did, however, present decisive points of view for its understanding.

2. However, this developmental view of the capitalistic mode of production and its interpretation as a historical formation—whose high flowering he observed—led Marx to the prognosis of its fall. He wanted to understand how or by what laws this fall would take place. This law is a special case of a general law, whereby a "mode of production"—that is, a total cultural period—develops its own antitheses and is cancelled out by these antitheses. This cancellation is to be understood in the Hegelian sense of a negation, which at the same time implies the maintenance and preservation of certain important elements of the old epoch in the development of the new. The decisive antithesis is between the social productive powers and the capitalistic form—i.e., private ownership of the means of production, through which these productive powers are driven forth and increased, but also hindered in their development.

The capitalist mode of production encounters a barrier in the development of productive powers. At a certain stage it falls into a state of conflict with its own task of increasing wealth in consumer goods. Seen historically, it is the means out of which develops the material productive power. Marx explicitly finds justification for the capitalistic mode of production in its historical calling, but it can fulfill its calling only if the capitalist makes the act of obtaining surplus value, as utilization of capital, the exclusive goal of production. This happens at the expense of the rest of society, especially of the working class, which becomes increasingly more numerous and, if these tendencies are not stemmed, increasingly more miserable. When rates of profit fall, the development of the productive power of labor creates a law which stands in opposition to the development of the capitalistic mode of production, in that it brings the capitalistic system to a point, where it becomes simply incompatible with its own content which is *"Vergesellschaftung"* of labor and the control of the means of production by the human intellect. The material conditions of a higher mode of production, the cooperative one, are then given.

How these cooperative forms come into existence and develop, Marx outlines merely in a few scattered notes. But he was convinced of one thing, which is the precondition for everything: The working class must and will fight for and gain political power. He meant the political power, and occasionally even mentioned that during the phase of the transition from the capitalistic to the socialistic mode of production, there would have to be a "dictatorship of the proletariat" (a phrase he uses several times). That he conceived this dictatorship to be based on democratic principles as a natural consequence of the democratic republic as the last and highest form of the bourgeois state can be seen not only from his other "dialectical" hypotheses but also from the form of his statements about them. For pure theory, the question of a "more brutal or more humane form," depending on the degree of development of the working class and the political system as such, is not of great importance. In the three hefty volumes of *Capital* the expression "dictatorship of the proletariat" is not found.

3. Evaluation and judgment of the capitalistic mode of production is closely linked with the view that it is including its origin and decline, a phenomenon which is historically determined. Classical political economics, because it views the basic forms as a natural necessity, sees in its present evolution nothing except the superiority a developed culture has over primitive conditions. The great expediency of the division of labor on a folk for the national economy as well as for the world economy, the great advantages of unfettered labor, free competition, free play of economic forces, benefits of sharp undertakings and speculations of negotiating traders and merchants who are able to predict needs and who, instead of the producer himself, take over the selling of products to distant markets, but at the same time work for the advantage of the producer, all this is seen in classical economics as products of enlightment. Also the benevolence of all these things benefit the capitalist, who on his part advances the worker his wages and grants him the use of the organization, the machinery, the

new inventions, while the worker again through his performance helps the capitalist to live up to his commitments. Herein
lie, as the economist sees it, the advantages of large-scale enterprises and all the innovations of economic life developed by
capital and labor. On the whole, the political economist sees in
this development only the light side contrasted with the dark
background of barbarian epochs and peoples, like the philosopher who views scientific enlightenment and rationality as
contrasted with the darkness of superstition.

In philosophy all this became questionable through the criticism arising out of romanticism of its offspring, codetermined
historical research. And, likewise, in the field of economics it
was the criticism of political economy which questioned previous views. Romanticism stresses the murky, even black, sides
of this developmental process. Soon it becomes evident that
the slavery and bondage of the past is replaced by a new kind
of servitude for labor. It is also evident that the relatively
happy and natural condition of one's work, and in which the
worker is united with the means of production on which private property was based, has vanished. It has given room, and
still is doing so, in a monotonous, hard, and difficult process, to
capitalistic private property, which steadily grows and brings
in its wake a mass of misery, oppression, and degeneration. At
the same time the indignation of the ever-growing proletariat
is steadily increasing.

The critic differs from the economist who eyes the future
with hesitation and doubts, fearing that the ignorance of the
masses caused by false communist teachings will bring about
the ruin of the capitalistic social order. The critic of political
economics sees in the future the realization and fulfillment of
all ideals because this future well-being is already present in
the achievements of the capitalistic era in the development of
the productive powers, in the cooperation, and in the social
enterprise which controls the forces of nature. The future salu-
tary conditions based on a completely new order, with the
common possession of land and of all means of production, will
arrive wherein individual freedom becomes the condition for
free development of all human beings, because freely socialized humans will take the material processes of production
under their conscious, planned control.

Thus, the critic of classical political economics shares with the economist (as well as with political liberalism and with the mainstream of modern philosophy) the point of view that there will be a steady advance of humanity in a straight line. They see such progress as fostered especially through science and technology of the newer age. However, classical economists see this progress also in the present social order, whose defaults and weaknesses they either misunderstand or see as nonessential or as attributable to human guilt and thus unavoidable, or else they believe them to be remediable and removable by means of continuing the traditional institutions, especially general education which they think might still be improved. Marx, on the other hand, sees the continuance of these institutions merely as a hindrance to progress. For him, the breakthrough of light may only come about by overcoming those institutions. Their collapse, which is approaching, alone will ensure the abolition of the root of all social evil; namely, the cleavage of the classes with one having dominance over the other. As much as Marx hated the control of the bourgeoisie and wished for its destruction, his theory, always keeps this postulate and even more so its ethical principles in the background. The theory merely predicts and concludes what will follow from the known premises.

4. But related to these premises is the insight that the existing order is not as harmonious a system as political economics had assumed in a more or less expressed way. To be sure, the explicit assumption originates in "vulgar economics" which sees nothing problematical in the relationship of sources of income. It feels at home "in the alienation produced as the various components of value face each other," because here it *seems* to be self-evident that rent belongs to the soil as its source, that interest belongs to capital as its source, and wages in the same way to labor. Vulgar economics separates and makes independent a given element which is also present in classical economics. However, classical economics struggles to eliminate this tendency in that it tries to comprehend the inner connections as distinct from the variety of its forms of appearance. Therefore, the last great representative and highest achiever of "classical" political economics, *Ricardo*, "conspicuously makes the antagonism between class interests, be-

tween wages and profit, and between profit and rent the starting point of his investigations." For Marx, these contradictions
or antagonisms are the bases of movements: contradictions
between profit and rent were the bases of the movement from
the feudal to the capitalist mode of production; contradictions
between wages and profit, the basis for the movement from
the capitalist to the socialist mode of production. The latter
movement is, like its predecessors since "Urkommunismus"
(primitive or original communism), is determined and conditioned by the *class struggle*. It is itself antagonistic and, therefore, transcends itself through its inherent contradictions,
which reflect themselves in this antagonism. Herein lies the
great theme by which Marx brings in historical development.
According to him, legal relationships, like the forms of the
state, cannot be comprehended from within themselves nor
from the so-called general development of the human spirit
(Geistes). They are rooted in the material conditions of living
in civil society *(bürgerliche Gesellschaft)* and the "anatomy"
of civil society is to be sought in political economy (the material
interpretation of history or theory of historical materialism).

5. In this sense, the *critique* of the political economy fights
for the proletariat in the same way that classical economics
fights for the capitalist class and expresses its ideology. The
ideologies are the intellectual weapons in the class struggle.
But there is one important difference. Disinterestedness is an
essential characteristic of science. The political economist can
only remain disinterested and faithful to science as long as he
studies the capitalistic order in its absolute and final form of
social production, during a time when the class struggle is
latent or undeveloped or limited to sporadic appearances.
These were conditions under which classical political economics existed in England. With the developed class struggle, the
higher, more correct scientific conscience changes over into
the criticism of political economics and, at the same time,
necessarily turns into criticism of the capitalistic social order
and its material economic basis.The specific development of
German society explains why on German soil all original
progression of "bourgeois" economics was impossible, but not
its critique. *Insofar as* this critique in a way "represents" a

class, it must represent the proletariat, whose historical calling is the overthrow of the capitalistic mode of production and the eventual abolition of classes.

6. But, as a science, the critique of classical economics is a direct continuation of the latter, whose methods and principles it takes over. Ricardo had drawn the ultimate conclusions in classical economics. Sismondi had put forth its questionable nature, thereby preparing the groundwork for the embryo of criticism, but *Marx* aimed to apply this critique to its highest form. This is the true intention of his theory on surplus value. For that reason, he put so much extensive work into the theory of surplus value, eager to lay open its whole development. In his systematic writings he constantly referred back to it. To him, it is an essential characteristic of classical economics that it acknowledges gain ("profit") and not interest as the actual income of capital, so that interest is seen merely as a consequence, or output, of profit. He also notes that Ricardo no longer sees rent as an independent form and as income which originates in the soil, but as derived from the higher profits which the market provides for agricultural products to those producers who enjoy more fertile or better situated fields.

Furthermore, the surplus value theory has in Ricardo and his school once and for all dissolved the value of commodities into the value of *labor*, its actual and original cost price. This conclusion is already implicit, although it is not expressly stated, that profit represents in essence the whole of value except wage labor, that indeed, the separation of value into labor wages and profit is the elementary fact of the capitalistic mode of production. But classical economics proceeds analytically: it starts with the given forms—the kinds of income—as premises and seeks to bring them back to their unity. Here analysis must necessarily be the basic method, while in a more sophisticated scientific approach the genetic aspects of evolutionary process in its diverse phases is made the main subject of research. Therefore, Marx uses the concept of "surplus value" synthetically as a conceptual prototype and shows the reasons for its division into all the kinds of income existing besides labor wages. This presentation is the content of the three volumes of *Capital*, the title of which could also be "surplus value." In its essence, it is a strict theoretical work of deductive national economics. The genetic procedure is to be understood as a form of *cognitive mapping* which has as its subject the genesis and the linkage of *concepts*.

7. This is the *dialectical method*. By its use, Marx wanted to drastically remove himself from the usual logical or, as Engels called it, the metaphysical mode of thinking. Both had borrowed the method from Hegel, although they did not want to follow Hegel's ideological paths of thought. They wanted merely to use the approach to understand the facts studied rigorously and realistically, facts which they recognize as becoming and having become and therefore in the flux of movement. According to them, the final form carries in itself the principle of its negation, the development of which prepares the former's death. Marx called this the rational core of the Hegelian method which had to be discovered in its mystical shell. Noting that his predecessors in political economics believed that there is a natural order of production and exchange, he wanted, like them, to find and describe the persisting regularities of the forms of production; but even more so, and above all else, he wanted to find and describe the law of their change, the laws of transition from one form into another, and the special lawlike regularity of each period. This was to be comprehended in the flux of the movement and not in terms of immutability and absoluteness in the sense that the natural laws are conceived by natural scientists (today we may say: had been conceived).

Now, as Marx conceived the development of the socioeconomic structure as a natural historical process and society itself as a changeable and steadily changing organism, it then implies that it was his idea that the dialectical method should also clarify and permeate natural science. The core of the dialectical comprehension of nature, according to Engels, is the knowledge that rigid antagonisms and differences as they happen in nature have only a relative validity. In reality, it is our reflections which carry into nature this rigidity and absolute validity. When Marx put the whole secret of his critical interpretation of economics into the conception that the labor which is present in commodities has a double character in that it produces simultaneously a concrete use value and an abstract value, then this is, as can be inferred, also to be understood dialectically; namely, in the developmental process of the capitalistic mode of production, labor, which at first is primarily a producer of use value, later becomes primarily a producer of exchange value.

The same dialectical view underlies his claim that "for the first time" labor wage has been depicted as an irrational phenomenon concealing a relationship. Dialectically, this then means that only apparently is labor bought and paid, but that actually it is the principle of the growth of values and their immanent measure. It has no worth of itself and is no commodity; it is the function of labor power and, therefore, represents labor power's use value. This labor power is bought by the capitalist, who thus becomes master of its use value, which seemingly is paid by the labor wage, but in reality this use value cannot be paid as *living* labor, except insofar as it is incorporated in values. These values are only paid insofar as they are absolutely necessary for the maintenance and reproduction of labor *power*. The dialectic is apparent in the view that on the one hand labor is paid, inasmuch as it reproduces the value of the labor power—and that at the same time, it is not paid—namely, insofar as it produces value beyond the value of the labor power. This phenomenon, the belief that the price of labor itself was contained in the labor wage, "forms the basis of all the legal notions of both laborer and capitalist, of all the mystifications of the capitalistic mode of production, of all its illusion as to liberty, of all the apologetic shifts of the vulgar economists."[1] And still, it is this phenomenon "which makes the actual relation invisible and, indeed, shows the direct opposite of that relation."[2] Evidently, this thought is to be supplemented by noting that the contradiction in this relationship is at the same time the chief point on which the development and thus the transformation of the capitalistic mode of production is dependent.

8. The critique is always conscious of its own position in the stream of development of theories and of this position's being conditioned by the development of things. The progress of theory is at the same time the decisive impetus to the opposi-

tion against the hitherto valid teaching. This opposition appears in a more or less economic, utopian, critical and revolutionary form, at first especially as utopian socialism —thus, like capitalistic political economics is itself a reflection of social development. The development of scientific thinking, and of the antithesis produced by it, keeps pace with the realistic development of the social antagonisms and class struggles contained in capitalistic production. Utopian socialism is, therefore, an expression of the proletarian consciousness at a time when the capitalistic mode of production was still undeveloped or today we would say with *Sombart:* at a time of transition from early capitalism to high capitalism. It is the first step of critical, or of scientific socialism, just as vulgar economics is, so to say, the last step of classical political economics, characterizing its decomposition, after it has "by its analysis dissolved its own premises."

The utopians want, in Engels' own words, to construct the elements of a new society out of their heads. They must proceed in this manner because these elements do not yet appear in a generally visible form in society. In considering the elementary forms of its new structure, they were thus limited to an appeal to reason, because they could not yet appeal to contemporary history. But history shows today—to continue with Engels' analysis—the contradictions of the capitalistic mode of production developed to such crying antagonisms "that the approaching breakdown can, so to speak, be grasped with one's hands." Only a new mode of production, corresponding to the present degree of development of the productive powers, is able to preserve these mighty new productive powers and develop them further. The struggle of both classes, which has arisen from the existing mode of production, has taken hold in all civilized countries and is becoming more vehement every day. An insight into this historical relationship, into the conditions of social reform made necessary by this class struggle, and likewise into the basic traits of this necessary reform, has already been obtained.

Thus, even when Marx finds his own mission and the mission of his theory to be that of elevating the unconscious striving of the proletariat of both worlds to a conscious thinking and to a clear perception of its task, he, nevertheless, does not presume the success of the intellectual class struggle as exclusively and decisively dependent on the reception and adoption of his theory. He specified the final goal of his work as that of uncovering the economic laws of change of modern society. He expected that the spread of this insight would produce a great strengthening of the proletariat in its inevitable struggle, in the fulfillment of its historical calling, but "even when a society has got upon the right track for the discovery of the natural laws of its movement . . . it can neither clear by bold leaps, nor remove by legal enactments, the obstacles offered by the successive phases of its normal development. But it can shorten and lessen the birth pangs."[3]

9. In the context in which these sentences appear—in the Preface to the first edition (1867) of *Capital*—they mean that the labor movement and the proletarian consciousness do not only, or by themselves, directly work toward the socialistic revolution. They also indirectly influence "society" ("the Gesellschaft") and thereby also influence the state, even though the society and the state stand in opposition to the labor movement, the proletariat, and the revolution. This agrees with other statements made at that time by Marx at the height of his career. In the inaugural address to the International Working Men's Association, written in September 1864, the misery of the masses was described in bold colors. This misery had not been alleviated by the improvement of machinery, nor by chemical discoveries, the application of science to production, the improvement of the communications media, nor by new colonies, emigration, free trade, nor by all these things considered together. He talks of the ever-increasing recurrence, the greater expansion and the deadly effect of the social *pest*—normally called industrial and commercial crisis. However, in this new manifesto to the working classes of Europe, Marx also talks with great decisiveness about the "bright side" of the development since the failure of the 1848 revolution. This development is featured by two great events which we are repeating here because of the great significance they have. The first: the ten-hours' bill (to read: the English ten-hour law) —whose great point of controversy was the struggle about the

lawful limitations of the working day. The crucial point of the controversy was between the blind domination of the law of supply and demand postulated by bourgeois political economics and the control of social production under laws of protection and justice demanded by the political economics of the working class.

The other great event is, according to Marx, an even larger victory for which the political economy of the working class has fought. "We speak of the cooperative movement, especially the cooperative factories raised by the unassisted efforts of a few bold 'hands.' " . . . "The value of these great social experiments cannot be overrated." . . . "By deed instead of by argument, they have shown that production on a large scale, and in accord with the behests of modern science, may be carried on without the existence of a class of masters employing a class of hands; that to bear fruit, . . . the means of production do not need to be monopolized as means of control over and as means of exploitation of the laborers themselves; furthermore, that, like serf labor, hired labor is but a transitory and inferior form, destined to disappear before associated labor plying its toil with a willing hand, a ready mind, and a joyous heart."[4] After a discussion of shortcomings which are necessarily a part of these worker experiments, Marx said: "To save the industrious masses, cooperative labor ought to be developed to national dimensions, and consequently, to be fostered by national means,"[5] and this can be accomplished only if the working class conquers political power.

For the present discourse, the only important thing is only the concession made by Marx that even at that time new and revolutionary factors were active in the bourgeois society which meant for him the "bright sides" of development. It is for this reason that the same thought was strongly emphasized in other places.

Marx said in his Preface that he gave so much space to such matters as the history, the substance, and the results of the English factory legislation, because one nation can and should learn from another. From this is to be concluded that, "apart from higher motives," it would be in the interest of the present ruling classes to clear away all legally controllable obstacles which hinder the development of the working classes. The process of revolution is palpable in England and at a certain high point it must carry over to the Continent.

It is peculiar that similar expressions of the above type made by Marx are not found in Engels' writings or only appear in feeble versions. Although he could so easily have spoken about the cooperative movement, only the transformation of the large production and transportation agencies into joint stock companies and state property proved to him that the bourgeoisie was unneeded for the management of modern productive powers. Only in the description of Owen's life did he mention the cooperative associations which since [Owen] have "at least" given the solid proof that the merchant, as well as the manufacturer, are very dispensable persons. Engels does not mention factory legislation. However, we are not dealing here with the differences between Engels' and Marx's modes of thinking.

Marx's statements to the effect that the legislation for the protection of the worker had been the first conscious reaction of society ("the Gesellschaft") against the tendencies of the capitalistic mode of production, that the wonderful development of the great branches of industry which are the very result of this legislation together with the physical and moral regeneration of the factory workers, had surprised "the dullest eye," indicate his position. He notes that by means of the legal regulation of the working day, the laborer is gradually overcoming the power of resistance of capital, while at the same time the offensive power of the working class is increasing by a great number of allies from social strata not directly involved in the struggle. Therefore, a comparatively rapid progress since 1860 has come about.[6]

Utterances such as these, and others, which glorify the victories of the workers' theory of national economics, stand in open contradiction to those powerful, oratorically bombastic statements about the growth of the amount of misery of the masses, of oppression, of slavery, of degeneration, of exploitation. They likewise stand in contrast to similar statements concerning the indignation of the steadily swelling working class, which is becoming schooled, united, and organized through the mechanism of the capitalistic production process.[7] From these utterances a special "theory of misery" *(Verelendungstheorie)* was developed. It was developed under probably earlier impressions, and other moods. Only thus can one reconcile this view with those insights which led Marx to calling the creation of a normal working day the product of a long-time, more or less hidden "civil war" between the capitalist class and the working class.[8] This "civil war" has, if the interpretation is correct, developed and progressed steadily without interruption until 1914 in England and especially also in Germany; and yet we look back on this period as a peaceful and happy time which, in Germany, was only interrupted by three short and relatively unimportant wars that were necessary for her national development. For England, too, as people will admit, the peaceful advance of the development toward socialism in both countries would have been more advantageous, however useful the destruction of German trade and the German fleet might have been for British economy and the empire.

Marx, in the often-cited Preface, predicts that the revolutionary process would move on the Continent in more brutal or in more humane forms, depending on the degree of development of the working class itself. And, indeed, this process today has without doubt taken on the most brutal and most hateful forms and not only in Russia and her neighboring countries. It can be confidently guessed that the hindrances to which the development of the lower strata in these countries had been submitted are one reason for this brutality. Although, of course, mere intellectual education does not prevent mad fanaticism either, and it can never be a substitute for a natural political mind, but instead contributes to the confusion of the mind as a *"Half or quarter education."* A mature political understanding is determined by profound knowledge; and the fruit borne in a healthy mind is moderation and circumspection which will always dominate even though the passionate movements in times of unrest may dissolve them and push them into the background.

10. In a most striking manner, and as the result of his profound studies, *Sombart* remarked that in Marx's teachings various basic ideas are confused and cannot be explained by a

holistic conception of ideas; in Marx the old revolutionary Adam keeps coming to the fore every so often and plays havoc with his laboriously acquired sociopolitical realism. Today Marx's authority is maintained and debated by young, credulous disciples as the Bible is by theologians. To them it is a self-evident premise that the absolute truth is contained therein, but this makes more sense in the case when the truth is thought of as representing "the word of God," than when the creed encounters much and superior disavowal. The disciples, however, are always merely concerned with the correct interpretation of the *"Ipse dixit,"* and, as is well known, the dispute over it can degenerate into bloody battles.

It should never be forgotten that in scientific considerations even of the most important writers, errors, contradictions, and weak reasoning are found. To be just to a man's theory or teaching, a student of it must focus attention on its healthy, ripe nucleus which the author himself can or might best justify before his own intellectual conscience. If in this light one considers the critical socialism founded by Marx, then the interpretation is certainly well-grounded that the gradual lawful transformation and evolution of the capitalist into the socialist or cooperative mode of production is not only generally wished by him, and in a humane ethical sense worth striving for (what he always denied, in order to let it be concluded from his presentations), but also portrayed as possible, if not even highly probable.

Marx certainly never stopped expecting and calling for political revolutions which would give the proletariat political power and, moreover, *dictatorial* power, in order to achieve the legal change from the old to the new order. Only in moments of dark anger and bitterness, from which this much beplagued and banned man could not free himself, may he have imagined and dreamed with satisfaction of the dictatorship as a "terror," as the rule of force (an expression of Engels) by which a small minority would stand at the head of unconscious masses. In the sense that he took seriously the Commune Uprising of 1871 and saw in it the first realization of such a dream "in a country in which hardly one single subjective or objective condition for a new order was fulfilled" ... (Sombart);

this surely must belong to the psychological and, as one must admit, to the pathological reactions of the man and the thinker Marx, but not to the pertinent and consistent understanding of his life's work.

NOTES AND REFERENCES

1. T.N.: Cap. I 591–92.
2. T.N.: Ibid.
3. T.N.: Ibid., pp. 14–15.
4. T.N.: S W I 383.
5. T.N.: Ibid., pp. 353–54.
6. T.N.: Cap. I 324.
7. T.N.: Ibid., p. 728.
8. T.N.: Ibid., p. 263.

Chapter 4

HISTORICAL MATERIALISM

To be sure, this lifework is only a fragment. The reader will remember that the four volumes of *Capital* were to be followed by research into ownership of land, wage labor, the state, foreign trade, and world market, to round out the critique of the political economy. Many other projects, partly of a philosophical character, kept Marx's mind busy, as has been mentioned. The fragmentary nature of some of his work was fateful for his lasting place in world literature, which became so extraordinary. Especially his theory of history, even though it was not necessarily a new one, was not well developed and indeed it was only tossed out as a hasty sketch. There is really no evidence to indicate that he intended to make a picture from the sketch. A mistake which the person unacquainted with Marx could easily make would be to assume that he meant to study history in the sense implied in the sketch and that he often tested the approach to see whether his theory held. In the four volumes of his letter-exchange with Engels, which lasted for nearly forty years, and which for half of this time (1852–1871) was never interrupted, the materialistic conception of history is never mentioned, even though Marx continually reported and discussed his studies and research.

In reality, the sketch on the materialistic conception of history meant nothing further for Marx than what he preferred to call in his younger years a "self-clarification"—that is, a settlement of accounts with his philosophical, ideological Hegelian consciousness, which dominated his thinking for a long time until he was led into new ways by Feuerbach. Significant theories are misunderstood when their background is not taken into account, and one is often not able to understand effectively a background because one is unable to measure the power by which the originators were bound to their predecessors and masters. But such understanding would be needed in order to evaluate correctly and adequately the energy which it took for the originators to break loose from their predecessors.

What does *Christian Wolf* and his school mean to us? And yet, for Kant the *Critique of Pure Reason* was essentially and mainly the renunciation of this school of Wolf's. What does Hegel mean to us? and the Hegelian Left? For Marx the materialistic conception of history was the renunciation of Hegel and the Hegelian philosophy of right, whose "criticial revision" was the first work in which Marx undertook to overcome the doubts which preoccupied him. Whoever carefully reads that criticism in the German-French *Yearbooks* will recognize this clearly. This struggle for freedom from Hegel may be seen by a comparison—that of the nature and tone of the "Contribution to the Critique of Hegel's Philosophy of Right" on the one hand, with the 1859 Preface on the other. Compared to the pathos and language of sparkling antitheses in the first, the Preface of 1859 is objective, scientifically rigorous, almost passive and not without elegance. In the first, the material basis of revolution is sought and demanded in the dissolution of society for the development of the proletariat, and that in order to materialize the latter's needs, theory will materialize itself, and ideas will hit the naive soul of the folk like strokes of lightning. In the Preface of 1859, the renunciation of the magical power of thought and of ideas has become almost complete. The belief in it was the inheritance of the Hegelian school and of classical, speculative, intellectualistic German philosophy in general.

The withdrawal from Hegel's idea meant a return to the predominant mode of thinking of the eighteenth century to which Kant also remained true to its contents in all important respects. Its bases to which Marx moved are natural science; it is the negation of the mythologically naive, and of the theological *Weltanschauung*. After the romantic period and theological restoration, which was also found in speculative philosophy, the nineteenth century returned to natural science, enriched by the introduction of the concepts of becoming and of organic development, which was formed in and is the mark of this romantic period. The nineteenth century thinks—in terms of natural science also—"historically." But this historical way of thinking is no longer that of epical history, not that of the hero-sagas and miracles; it no longer sees the mirror-image of God in humans. This historical view of humanity no longer sees mankind as wandering through the desert of its fate according to God's command and destiny; or which, having lost paradise through disobedience, is saved through God's grace and, according to the sayings of sibyls and prophets, hastens toward its end in the fourth and last *Weltreich;* and there anticipates the millenium which, under the leadership of the reappearing Christ, shall finally conquer the anti-Christ, to be then redeemed on the last day, the Day of Judgment. Rather, the new historical, anthropological way of thinking sees an image of nature in the human, who in the course of hundreds of thousands, even millions of years has become like other organic beings and, in a steady struggle with nature, has developed intellect and knowledge. It sees in man a species which increases in numbers and gradually expands in space through experience and through the use of tools, especially through the care of the soil and the taming of wild animals as helpers. It sees man, who has created *culture* through the formation of *language,* as a means of communication and mutual understanding, and whose *religion,* as the intercourse with past and imagined powers, gives him courage and comfort. Thus, it sees in man's history, the development of intellect, the learning of the arts, especially the arts of plowing and sowing fields and building houses. Man then has climbed up from crude and savage conditions, has ennobled himself and developed to his present state still highly deficient but, nonetheless, capable of further progress. Not in the past, but in the future, it invisages man's perfect form of existence.

Man went through struggles and wars from the very beginning; he made weapons and improved them like other tools. Up to this very hour people live side by side in much enmity as well as in peaceful intercourse; they hurt, destroy, and subject each other; but striving is directed increasingly and predominantly toward agreement and unity. And is it not thought which furthers, guides, and characterizes human striving, just as the animal is guided through its senses and instincts? Is not the human spirit the same thing as the free will of the human? Romantic philosophy asks these questions and would like to answer them in the affirmative. Scientific philosophy lets the affirmative stand conditionally; but negates with great emphasis the belief in any absolute cleavage separating animal from human; it acknowledges free will as an idea which is identical with practical reason, but not as something exempt from a necessary connection with nature; when reality is researched, only then is determinism the bitter fruit of truth.

Marx intended to ascertain the natural laws of human development. Hegel had, despite his amphigoric language, so developed his system that even the part of his school from which Marx came, understood him to mean that it is the absolute free spirit which is ruling history and especially, as an objective spirit, manifests itself in religion, and that it is the task of philosophy to translate religious truth from feeling into reason. Feuerbach taught that the absolute spirit is the deceased spirit of theology, which was still ghosting around in Hegelian philosophy. But for Hegel the absolute spirit also realizes itself in the state. He does not conceive it theologically, but wholly ideologically; for him it is the reality of the moral idea which has as its basis the law as reality. Human intelligence is looked at and admired in these phenomena. The view contained in the rationalistic mode of the enlightenment that the intellect is the essence of the human being, that from within himself man formed such creations as right and state, and that from within himself he is called to form them anew is not without contradiction to its anthropological bent. This illusion also belonged to the heritage of theology and religious illusions.

Marx wanted to say this in his essay of 1843 in which he intends to unmask "self-alienation" in its "unholy forms" after its "holy forms" were unmasked by Feuerbach's critique. Marx was saying that for him the criticism of religion changes into the criticism of right, the criticism of theology into the criticism of politics. These thoughts were still molded in the forms of Hegelian philosophizing. Sixteen years later these forms are shed, but the basic thought structure remained. The criticism focuses on ideological representations, whether of Hegelian or of liberal enlightened origin, and opposes the assumption that the human spirit is floating freely in the air and, according to its own essence, arranges the civilization of nations and that, therefore, correct thinking, and correct understanding will in all instances always bring about the right organization of life. The realistic view which Marx sets against these opinions is in its essence related to two other important theorems which dominated a mighty field of thought in the second half of the nineteenth century and from which they can only be expelled by external force.

The first of these theorems is the "voluntaristic" view of the human soul[1] contained in Schopenhauer's theory of the will, which taken from its metaphysical frame maintains its psychological truth. Even though Marx and Schopenhauer were and remained far apart from each other [Marx was born in the year of the publication of *The World as Will and Idea (Die Welt als Wille und Vorstellung*, 1819)], one can nevertheless understand with good reason Marx's "historical materialism" as an application of Schopenhauer's theory of the will. Thus, for both theorists it is not the conscious, but rather the unconscious spirit or will which is the decisive power for social life, as well as for the life of individuals. Not reason but a darkling drive, not thought but need is "the prime mover," the original power in the life of a human and in human development. Here are the "material life relationships," the circumstances under which people make life possible for themselves. Thus, they get food by hunting, fishing, gathering of wild fruits and tubers, and agriculture, producing for their lives through their own work. They enter, says Marx, "into relations that are indispensable and independent of their will." He preferred to call these production relationships; they "correspond to a definite stage of development of their material forces of production."

This is to say: Relationships are different under simple conditions when humans live in caves or tents in nonregulated unions or hordes and hew stones; they are different when humans have learned to melt iron ore and forge weapons in strictly organized cooperative sexual unions, when they build plowshares from wood and iron; they are different when humans build stone houses and wood ships which can be steered

rudders or even by wind caught in sails; finally they a\
ent, after the invention of powder, the compass, the sp\
machine, the mechanical loom, the steam engine, etc.\
The increasing density and condensation of living condit\
is the result; the division of labor, of occupations, separation\
management and labor, of masters and slaves, of villages an\
towns spreads and diversifies civilization. Masters think differently than servants, lords differently than commoners, peasants differently than burghers—why? Because they cultivate
different life-styles, life-habits, and customs; they cultivate
these because they have different needs and diverse possibili-
ties to satisfy them. "It is not the consciousness of men that
determines their being, but, on the contrary, it is their social
being that determines their consciousness."[2] Couched in the
language of Schopenhauer, this sentence would read : will, as
the blind, darkling drive for self-maintenance and sexual reproduction, has primacy over self-consciousness; intellect is
this will's servant and tool. Schopenhauer could also have concluded that in the history of culture, the wish decides as the
father of the thought; the interest, as the guider of opinions,
the need and the desire as the spur of inventive thought.

The other important theorem which Marx touches is the
theory of evolution. The version of *Lamarck*, which Marx does
not seem to have known, would have corresponded even more
closely to his own ideas than that of Darwin. *Darwin*, he says
in a note,[3] has "interested us in the history of nature's technology, i.e., in the formation of the organs of plants and animals, which serve as instruments of production for sustaining
life—(Lamarck had done this in a much more meaningful
way). Does not the history of the productive organs of man, or
organs that are the material basis of all social organization,
deserve equal attention?"

In the following an effort is made to complete the content
of those sentences written by Marx in the Preface of 1859 in
which revolutions and their causes are mentioned. Others and
especially Engels have tried to do this. According to the Preface, the productive organs, which may be compared to the
vegetative organs of the animal organism, bring about property relationships which are the basis for production relation-

ships in the same way as the animal has its sense and motor organs. They are their developmental forms and serve them as such, but when the productive organs—i.e., the technical capabilities and the productive power of labor—develop to a higher degree, then the developmental forms become fetters. The former, that is to say those vegetative organs, need different, newer, improved animal organs, that is, they call for a different law, different property relationships, a different idea-world. Gradually—slower or faster—the latter follow the transformation of the former. Men are becoming aware of the conflict of the contradiction between productive powers and property relationships and between vegetative and animals organs. This awareness is reached through judicial, political, religious, artistic or philosophical, in short, ideological forms, and men even fight the conflict out in these forms. Here the analogy with prehuman organisms is no longer sufficient, only the human himself presents these forms. In the last instance his intellectual life is dependent upon his vegetative life; his consciousness is determined by his being, his thinking, his wishes, and his interests; his idea-life is directed by his will. Like the social institutions and the law, the intellectual life is a "superstructure" which rises from the "material basis." Better stated, they are organs which are nourished from the life stream and the contradictions, struggles, and revolutions, which are in the material basis, are followed by contradictions, struggles, and revolutions in the whole monstrous "superstructure." The technical, economical, industrial revolutions bring political and intellectual revolutions in their wake.

The means which Marx and Engels, as disciples of German philosophy, use to distinguish themselves from all natural scientists and from *Schopenhauer,* whom they must have scorned as an unsuspecting metaphysicist (they do not seem to have known him) is the *dialectic.* The dialectic was to be the means for understanding and grasping that which is becoming and changing. The thought or belief that that which is becoming, already is, even if in a negated or hidden condition, like the embryo, or better like the ovum in the mother's womb, is maintained in the dialectic. The analogy holds for the expression, that the material conditions of existence of the new state or higher production relationships are "hatched" in the womb of the old society. Only then do they take the place of the former societal order which has developed all the productive powers for which it is sufficiently matured. The tasks which face humanity, which it postulates for itself, can only come into being where the material conditions for their solution are already in existence or are at least in the process of becoming.

We are here reminded of the simile that the "Capitalist integument is burst asunder,"[4] that the pangs of birth can be shortened,[5] etc. Marx believed and taught that with this *temporis partus maximus* a great turning point arrives—the end of "prehistory" of human society. Engels called it a leap from the realm of necessity into the realm of freedom. It was to bring with it the abolition of all classes and of all class domination; the last antagonistic form of the social production processes, insofar as this form grows out of the social living conditions of individuals, was thereby to be overcome.

Marx sees the methods of production, and thus, the epochs of the social economic structure, as progressive, as linear, and as the main content of world history, or rather of prehistory; "in broad outlines" he designates the Asiatic, the ancient, the feudal and the modern bourgeois (capitalistic) modes of production as such epochs. Have the developments and the transitions from one epoch into another really happened in such a form in accordance with his theory? As far as we know, Marx never bothered to investigate this. Only one great parallel is always in front of him. This is the development of the capitalistic mode of production and its corresponding "superstructure" from the feudal mode of production and from its ideological forms; the class struggle and the revolutions, which have filled the last centuries are to a certain extent still to be experienced and observed. On the other hand, the foreseen, the wholly and truly fore*seen* death of this economic structure, the creation of a new socialistic world with its own ideas, the class struggles inherent in this creation, and the great revolutionary turning point—which was awaited—that already was the theme of the *Communist Manifesto*—it was the guiding thought of his life, the guiding thread in his studies.

But the *dialectic* plays yet a special role in these studies and in his historical-philosophical thinking which was not brought out in the much cited part of the Preface (1859). Here is meant the concept of *synthesis* specific to the Hegelian logic; synthesis combining both the preceding thesis and antithesis, which means at the same time a restoration and a renewal. In the broadest version it is to be understood as a "negation of the negation."[6] Accordingly, there are always three acts in this profession.[7] (1) Modern development, whose diagnosis is the great task of the criticism of political economy: The capitalistic mode of production is *negation*—negation of individual private property based on one's own labor. It develops its own negation out of a process inherent in nature, the negation of the negation thus reestablishes private property. "This does not reestablish private property for the producer, but gives him individual property based on the acquisitions of the capitalist era, i.e., cooperation and the possession in common, of land and of the means of production."[8] (2) Communal property, which is the original basis of modern development, is to be restored. From it, the development started—into it, it will flow. Here all of civilization with its private property of land and tools, its money economy, its trade and usury profits, appears long *before* the capitalistic mode of production, as a negation of the original conditions of "freedom, equality, and brotherhood in the old tribes." Lewis Morgan depicted them in his *Ancient Society*, which was based on his life with the Iroquois Indians, and Marx took account of this. He had previously found in the "extraordinarily important" books of G. L. von Maurer the proof for his own point of view—although Maurer did not know of this—that everywhere in Europe the Asiatic and the Indian forms of property were the beginning.

One could not maintain that these two presentations of the negation and synthesis are completely compatible with each other, but neither Marx nor Engels was aware of the ambivalence and the difference, otherwise traces of trying to unite them would have been left in their works. Nowhere is it stated clearly whether private property per se or only the capitalistic private property is the target of Marx's analysis; whether the simple production of commodities or only the capitalistic production of commodities are the "crazy forms" in which the social relationships of persons appear "masked" in the social relationships of things and of products of labor. Nowhere are we told whether the Asiatic, ancient, and feudal social structures have or primarily and exclusively the capitalistic structure the above-mentioned characteristics of negating the natural relationship of persons to persons and of persons to things which is to be preserved in a union of free men where people work with the communal cooperative means of production and invest their many individual labor powers consciously as social labor power, and where the relations of people to their labors and their labor products again become transparently simple and remain so "in the production as well as in the distribution." Nor are we told whether it is only in the capitalistic epoch or in the previous ones that private property gives to commodities a mystical fetish character, which inherently insists that the relations appear as material relationships of persons and as social relationships of things, that is, not as that which they are. Like astronomers and indeed, like all real scientific thinkers, Marx always tried assiduously to find and establish the real facts and the real movements as opposed to the apparent facts and the apparent movements.

NOTES AND REFERENCES

1. Masaryk and Tugan-Barnowsky expressly pointed to this before I did; the notice of it is already to be found in my preface (1887) to *Gemeinschaft und Gesellschaft*, 1st edition.
2. T.N. S W I 363. The oft-used quotations above this note in the text are also in the Preface here cited.
3. T.N.: Cap. I 406.
4. T.N.: Ibid., p. 837.
5. T.N.: Ibid. p. 15.
6. T.N.: Ibid., p. 837.
7. T.N.: The reader may follow Tönnies' train of thought if we insert here [in the two forms of modern development now to be mentioned].
8. T.N.: Cap. I 837.

Chapter 5

CRITIQUE

Did Marx succeed in establishing the real facts: That is the great question, particularly with regard to the economic and social problems; innumerable authors attempted to answer it by writing entire volumes or elaborate treatises. Our present endeavor can and should only be to offer a summary contribution thereto.

1. The value and surplus value theory stipulates that for the commodity which is meant to be exchanged there must be a measure of the value by which it is normally exchanged. This measure is provided by the amount of labor which was required or (to be more exact) which ought to have been required in the course of production of the commodity. This theory assumes that the total amount of labor represents the utility value of the purchased labor power. It neglects to point out that the buyer, that is, the entrepreneur or capitalist, also contributes value-producing labor to a commodity. Yet the theory assumes as a rule that the entrepreneur or capitalist is at the same time the production manager, so to speak, the head of the total labor force. He is often spoken of as the really active factor, particularly in cooperative processes. Furthermore, it is acknowledged that management is a special function belonging to "the capitalist" which arises out of the peculiar "nature of the social labor-process."[1] Marx adds that "it is at the same time a function of the exploitation of a social labor-process, and is consequently rooted in the unavoidable antagonism between the exploiter and the living and laboring raw material he exploits." The manager, as such, is compared to a conductor of a band or orchestra. "A single violin player is his own conductor; an orchestra requires a separate one. The work of directing, superintending, and adjusting becomes one of the functions of capital from the moment that labor, under the control of capital, becomes cooperative."[2]

Marx, in fact, assumes (especially in the conclusion to the *Theories of Surplus Value*) that in industrial profit, in distinction from interest, a "supervision wage" is included. "Capital in the production process appears as the director of labor, as commander of it *(captain of industry)* and thus plays an active role in the work process itself. But insofar as these functions arise from the specific form of the capitalist production, ... this kind of labor, which is a part of exploitation, *enters into the value of the product just as well as that of the wage laborer. This is exactly as in slavery where the labor of the supervisor of the slaves* has to be paid, as well as that of the laborers themselves."[3] He then develops this further: "the labor wage which is earned by the industrial capitalist stands in an opposite relationship to the amount of capital. It is considerable with small capitals because there the essence of the capitalist stands in the middle between exploitation of foreign labor and living off his own labor, while the supervision wage tends to vanish with huge capital or even become completely divorced from it when a director is employed."[4] "The capitalist mode of production has brought matters to a point where the work of supervision, entirely divorced from the ownership of capital ... being always readily obtainable ... is walking the streets."[5] [The last four words were in the German but not the English translation.] "There is no longer any reason why this work of management should be carried out by capitalists. It is quite realistically contained in capital ... in the separation of industrial directors, etc., from all kinds of capitalists. The best proof for this is given by the cooperative factories erected by laborers."[6] But basically, Marx's theory considered this supervisory labor as not existing; on the contrary, it is assumed that capital and labor are always separated from each other, and that capital appears exclusively and necessarily as a *buyer* of labor power, that it never possesses any labor power itself.

This abstraction taken by itself furthers conceptual knowledge. The abstraction, however, needs to be corrected by noting that it is merely a conceptual truth and nothing else. The question which inevitably arises is whether or not the work of management and supervision—be it connected with "exploitation" or bought for its own purpose—produces surplus value and, thus, is partly surplus *labor.* This question is not even posed by Marx. He seems to answer in the negative when he makes the following statement: "When comparing the mode of production of independent peasants and artisans with the production by slave labor, the political economist counts this labor of superintendence among the *faux frais de production.*"[7] (But, when considering the capitalistic mode of production he treats, the control functions made necessary by the cooperative character of the labor process as identical with the control functions necessitated by the capitalistic and, thus, antagonistic, character of that process.) Indeed, according to this theorem, one would have to say that this supervising labor, insofar as it is exploitation, is unessential and produces no value, but insofar as it is essential, it does produce value, therefore also surplus value. We may say that consequently the entrepreneur also produces surplus *labor* for himself if the value produced by him is larger than the value of his own labor input.

2. A radical error is closely connected with this ambiguity. Although Marx wanted to conceptualize the capitalistic mode of production as a historical phenomenon and desired to describe its development as arising from a precapitalistic mode of production, his basic concepts do not give evidence of such a historical view nor of a dialectical approach by which such a view should become manifest. He did not want to consider surplus labor for capital as something eternal; but, in his view, surplus labor in favor of capital is only preceded historically by surplus labor in favor of *other* owners of the means of production *who are also separated from labor;* as such, he considers the owners of slaves and the masters of serfs.[8] And yet, historically the expropriation of the folk masses from the land and soil—that is, from their essential means of production —formed the "basis" for the capitalistic mode of production. Indeed, the main theme is the destruction of private property resting on one's own labors, "the expropriation [of peasants and artisans] (e.g., the great mass of the people) from the soil, from the *means of subsistence,* and from the *means of labor;* this fearful and painful expropriation of the mass of the people forms the prelude to the history of capital . . . Self-earned

private property, so to say, is based on the fusion of the isolated, independent laboring individual with his private property based on the conditions of his labor, is supplanted by
capitalistic private property."[9] This theme is often repeated in
Marx's writings.

Here, especially, would have been the place to apply the
dialectical method in order to evaluate and measure the pertinent concepts and to study all the transitions from the crafts
(to mention only this one type of industrial production) to the
factory; from the master craftsman to the head of an enterprise
within abstract capital; from the condition in which one relies
on the revenue of one's own labor and *surplus labor* and in
which perhaps the "journeyman" may help, but may not contribute necessarily to surplus labor (because the master may
have enough surplus labor in his own labor), to the condition
in which one's own labor (and therefore surplus labor) ceases
to be necessary. Activity is limited to getting others to work in
that it now belongs to the *nature* of business to put purchased
labor power to longer and more work than would be justified
when considering the value of the laborers and the wages paid
to them.

Although the first volume of *Capital* is abounding in historical descriptions the emergence of the capitalistic mode of production is presented merely as the result of the so-called original accumulation. This is done, moreover, rather one-sidedly,
without drawing any conclusions from this for his basic concepts. One may take such a monumental work as *Sombart's
Kapitalismus* (especially the second edition) for a more complete picture, although even here the "being and becoming of
capitalism" has only been sketched and the question of surplus
value is not even mentioned. But for Marx this is the pivotal
question. Especially the "middle thing" between "exploitation
of other's labor and living off one's own labor," mentioned
cursorily, should have been for Marx an object of very special
theoretical interest. But the problem practically does not exist
for him at all.

3. Tied closely to this basic error is another one which is a
central part of the theory of value. The literature often mentions the allegedly unresolvable contradiction between the
value theory and the independence of the rate of profit from

the "organic relationship" of capital (although the latter is only abstracted from the variable part). According to Marx: the capitalists divide among themselves the whole surplus value in proportion to their *total* capital as cause and consequence of their competition among each other. The rate of profit, although originating in the surplus value, is not distributed proportionally to the various contributing capitals. Although all of them contributed a certain amount of surplus value, that is the surplus value produced by *their* respective laborers, the rate of profit originates in the relation between the total surplus value and the total capital. The profit rate thus calculated is then added to the cost price of each capital, whereby the production price of each capital is reached. This leads to an explicit denial of Marx's original premise that goods are exchanged according to their value: only in exceptional cases is the price of production identical with the value, normally it is either higher or lower.

That we have here a contradiction which demands the unthinkable to be thought has been unjustly maintained; however, we do have here a contrived, artificial, and inherently improbable mental construct. It is based on Marx's assumption that, first, value originates (as mentioned) exclusively in labor —partly paid and partly unpaid—provided by laborers not owning any property and thus, not owning capital. Second, he assumes that the produced commodity incorporates parts of the old value consisting of raw materials and means of production, as if the newly created value was merely added mechanically and externally to those parts of the old value; the whole being a simple arithmetical problem. It is absolutely inconceivable for Marx to see that living labor, when working on some kind of material and when being made more effective by means of tools and machines, will increase the value of this material and of these production means so that they will all augment their effectiveness and thereby, so to say, multiply each other instead of just forming a mere sum. This is unthinkable for Marx but not unthinkable per se, rather, it is quite probable and is confirmed by experience.

Also, the independence of the rate of profit from the proportionate part of capital invested in labor power is then something which is self-evident. I say, the independence, and that it generally also results from the value of the tools whose value is multiplied by labor because the "average rate of profit" is in reality composed of very diverse elements which are higher or lower according to the market demand for the products, the degree of dominance on the market or the monopolistic tendency, and the improbability or probability of competition. Why should not the same working time produce differing amounts of value depending on the kind of materials and the kind of tools that are used?

4. According to Marx's deduction, capitalistic production is a special case of trade (formula M - C - M'), just as usury is another special case (formula M - M'). How trade is possible if commodities are equal and remain equal in value, has not been made clear by Marx, as will be shown shortly. Indeed, trade is possible only because and insofar as the value of one and the same commodity *varies* according to the time and the place of the market and the fluctuating circumstances which act upon the utility value of the commodity, that is, upon its "marginal utility." Thus, the product of the isolated worker needing nourishment is of much less value to him than to the merchant who knows how to find a purchaser for it. This is even truer in the case of an isolated man's pure working power which a merchant is able to use in the production of value by joining it with the working power of other men and fitting them all into his array of machinery. So, indeed, labor power will create "more value", i.e., surplus value, than it has "value" in itself. An individual laborer's value is low without cooperation or unless he combines his labor power with that of others, unless he is given a chance to bring to the fore the skill and intelligence he happens to possess; he is feeble in the face of the powers of nature and of culture, whose powers are united in the hands of the entrepreneurial merchant, which force him, the laborer, to enter their system.

The entrepreneur "is at liberty to set the one hundred men to work without letting them cooperate."[10] "He pays them the value of one hundred independent labor powers, but he does not pay for the combined labor power of the hundred. Being independent of each other, the laborers are isolated persons who enter into relations with the capitalist, but not with one another. Cooperation begins only with the labor process, but laborers have then ceased to belong to themselves. On entering that process, they become incorporated within capital. As cooperators, as members of a working organism, they are but a special mode of the existence of capital. *The productive power developed by the laborer, insofar as he is a socialized laborer, is thus the productive power of capital.* This power is developed gratuitously whenever the workmen are placed under given conditions, and it is capital that places them under such conditions."[11] All these propositions are correct, but Marx did not draw any conclusions from them. He acknowledges expressly that not only trade, but also "merchant's capital is older than the capitalist mode of production and is, in fact, historically the oldest free state of the existence of capital."[12] He discusses how the independent development of merchants' capital stands in a reverse relationship to the degree of development of capitalistic production, that within the latter it is demoted from its former independent existence to a special momentum of the capitalistic establishment as such. For, once "the" capital became master of the production process, merchants' capital was forced to subordination and thus appeared merely as a form of capital with some *specific* functions. However, Marx forgets that there is no essential difference between the capital which gains power over production and any other kind of capital, with the exception perhaps of loan capital. Merchants' capital is precisely "the" capital to which production becomes subordinate.

Therefore, it is strange how Marx reconciles himself with his explanation of merchants' profit. He derives it very awkwardly and artificially as he declares that merchants' capital in a developed capitalistic mode of production is a dependent form of that part of industrial capital which is circulating, which produces no value and thus also no surplus value; Marx claims that merchants' capital receives a certain amount of surplus value from industrial capital by way of the laborers who work for the merchant. These laborers of the merchant *("Commis")* are supposed to cause this *transfer* and, *thus,* to be the reason for his profit. Since the size of the merchant's capital has an economizing influence, the use of wage labor has the same effect on its functions. Therefore, "commercial labor," purchased by merchants' capital, is productive for the latter; that is, it produces profit because the counting-house *(Kontor)*, which is its workshop, serves as a representative of industrial capital in that it provides for the realization of value, thus also of surplus value.

In the same way, banking capital is explained as a bifurcation of merchants' capital and the profit derived from it (while the interest on loan capital always appears as a diminution of profit without relation to labor and as a mere relationship between capitalists). Even if this explanation of trade profit were valid for the condition of modern society, where "industry dominates trade," what kind of explanation could be given for the situation in earlier times when industrial capital had not yet been in power?

"Since the movement of merchants' capital is M - C - M', a merchant's profit is made, first, in acts which occur only within the circulation process, hence in the two acts of buying and selling; and second, in the last act, in *sale*. It is, therefore, 'profit upon alienation.' "[13] How is this possible on Marxian premises? *"Prima facie*, a pure and independent commercial profit seems *impossible* as long as products are sold at their value. (Which is assumed to be the rule?) To buy cheap in order to sell dear is the rule of trade. Hence, not the exchange of equivalents. The conception of value is included in it, insofar as the various commodities are all values, and therefore money. In respect to quality they are all expressions of social labor. But they are not values of equal magnitude. The quantitative ratio, in which products are exchanged, is at first quite arbitrary. They assume the form of commodities inasmuch as they are exchangeables, i.e., expressions of one and the same sale. Continued exchange and more regular reproduction for exchange reduces this arbitrariness more and more, but at first not for the producer and consumer, but for their go-between, the merchant, who compares money-prices and pockets the difference. It is through his own movements that he establishes equivalence."[14] In other words, Marx must admit that capital profit does not alone and foremost originate in the sphere of production but also, and earlier, in the sphere of circulation. He reconciles himself with this fact, which does not fit into his system, by mentioning it only vaguely and by pointing out that commercial profit in an "exchange of products between undeveloped societies, . . . not only *appears* as outbargaining and cheating, but also largely originates from them. . . . Merchant's capital, when it holds a position of dominance, stands everywhere for a system of robbery and (plundering)."[15] As if he had not depicted the effects of industrial capital in the same light as "dripping from head to foot, from every pore, with blood and dirt!"[16]

Yet Marx would admit that trade and industrial capitalism are not *by nature* bound to be full of shame. "My standpoint, from which the evolution of the economic formation of society is viewed as a process of natural history, can less than any other make the individual responsible for relations whose creature he socially remains, however much he may subjectively raise himself above them," he writes in the so-often cited "Author's Preface" of 1867.

5. The essence of capitalism—if we may correct Marx's presentation—is the essence of trade. As we see it, capitalism is a more developed, more powerful, and more expanded form of trade. Even though strenuous activity may be connected with and often actually is involved in trade, there is not only a difference, but an obvious contrast between work or labor on the one hand, and trade on the other. Both are functions of social life, but labor is (if I may insert my concepts here) determined by community (Gemeinschaft) and natural will, trade by society (Gesellschaft) and rational will. Labor wants a reward for its achievements: either directly as a fruit for its endeavors or indirectly by means of exchange; trade wants to obtain "advantage" merely by means of repeated exchange, that is, it wants to harvest the fruits of labor without having performed the labor. Labor wants to produce concrete value: it wants things which sustain, advance, and adorn the life of the working person; trade wants to gain abstract value, which is inconsiderate of any of the purposes of the concrete values, and instead merely pursues the objective of its own perpetual accumulation. Labor wants *equal value* (equivalents) through

simple exchange; trade wants *surplus value* through double exchange.

When trade "takes possession of production" it gains a sphere which is essentially independent of the fluctuations on the markets which normally are the object of speculation of the merchant, as well as his risk, which he must try to cover. But this independence is not absolute since the commodities are still dependent on the markets. Compared to normal big trade, big industry is relatively solid and safe. When Marx says: "The real science of modern economy only begins when the theoretical analysis passes from the process of circulation to the process of production,"[17] one may agree with him, but one has to stress all the more that the statement: trade subordinates production (Marx's own expression), must be understood to mean that the production process *becomes* permanently linked with the circulation process.

So it is indeed, and this in a double sense. On the one hand, trade may leave the mode of production unchanged and show no other interest in technical matters than perhaps to lend tools and raw materials to the worker; in this case, the merchant remains an agent, a dealer, either by cooperating with the foremen or by directly "taking" the product from the worker. On the other hand, the merchant may himself become a producer (if the producer becomes a merchant, the same situation is given), in which case he may participate in the production of value by being an organizer, technical director, intellectual author. However, seen from the vantage point of trade, this is something purely accidental (the case of a master craftsman organizing his business in a commercial manner would be looked upon quite differently). The merchant, as such, only wants to use his capital in buying and selling and for him the production process is merely an outward, external means serving this goal. For a horse dealer a comparable situation exists when he considers both the pasture he rented for his young horses and the arsenic he feeds them as such external means serving his goals.

The production process serves to increase the value of the elements which are brought and mixed together within it: raw materials, machinery, labor power. The same is true when a grain-dealer mixes various kinds of rye or when a wine-dealer mixes good and poor wine, adds alcohol, sugar, etc. (these and other traders often change into "producers" without, however, receiving praise for that). In the wholesale and retail trade the processes of mixing and blending always have great significance. However, if one considers the production process as such a means, there is an important difference insofar as among the elements brought together there is one element which is not only a cause or a reason for the increase of value of the others (like sugar for the sour wine), but which is the cause of value as such, one element which is the value-producing *principle:* this element is labor power—and more precisely the combined labor power of several workmen whose productivity is tremendously increased beyond the productivity of a single workman by means of cooperation and the appropriate distribution and use of technical means.

For the merchant, there is as a rule no cheaper purchase than when he "manufactures" the commodities himself. He can manufacture them if he is able to "advance" the capital (whether he borrowed it or whether it is his own) to purchase the raw materials, the means of production, and labor power. Labor power is *for him* a mere auxiliary means, and he wants to purchase it only as such. The workers' labor is *for him* merely service or assistance. He is the intellectual author (although not the manager) of the production process, the master in the shop, the master over the means of production, the commander of the workmen. He stands like a colonel above his mercenaries, he is the owner of the resulting products, he is like a general who won the battle.

The degradation of the laborers, including those who are experienced and skilled, to the level of mere servicemen is the unavoidable result of the fact that they are not masters over the market and they no longer have control over cooperation and over the mass tools to which technical progress has made them servants. By uniting they may be able to maintain, or even to increase the price for their efforts, but they cannot decide about the true value of their achievements as long as they are deprived of the necessary institutions; in other words, as long as capital faces them as an alien or even hostile power.

Only to the extent that laborers themselves accumulate capital, which is large enough to carry the risks of a commercial operation, will they be in a position to call the revenue of their labors their own. However, exactly like a rational merchant, they should then only use a certain part for unproductive consumption. The rest must be saved for the renewal of deteriorated means of production, for the continuation and (perhaps) the expansion of production, for insurance against accidents and other interruptions of labor, including the necessity of taking care of unproductive laborers out of the "consumption fund."

Marx is right in stating that labor, the value-producing element and the yardstick for all other values, has in itself no value. But labor *power* has no value either (and it is a very far-fetched notion that its value is equal to the value of the foodstuffs, etc., which are produced by labor). Labor power has not been produced, it is no commodity, but like many other exchangeable objects it is treated as if it were a commodity and as if it had value. It only has a price and a quasi-value whose estimation is dependent on labor and demand by the owner of labor power, i.e. by the laborer himself, and by the one who wants to use it. However, the value of a real commodity is, of course, conditioned by the kind and amount of labor *incorporated* in it, insofar as labor power is necessary for its reproduction and depending on the conditions of the market. The laborer cannot successfully determine the price for his labor power which would correspond to the actual output achieved through cooperation with other labor power, since the capitalist "does not pay for the combined labor power of the hundred." However, coalitions with other workmen will help him to come closer to this price. Much less is he able to determine the price of his labor which would correspond to the actual output of labor after having made use of the perfectionalized means of production which are in the possession of capital. The *productivity* of labor remains latent and a mere potentiality as long as labor is not able to use these means of production, and it is capital which places them at labor's disposal.

6. A clear conceptual distinction must be made between production for the market—that is, for an anonymous buyer,

and production for one's own—Gemeinschaft-like—needs. This analytical distinction is necessary, although both are deeply involved in the whole problem of the relationship between capital and labor. Marx does not deal with this at all, not even when mentioning cooperative production. The producers' cooperative as such remains essentially competitive, and therefore easily reverts into a joint-stock-company, which is the most perfect form a purely commercially oriented enterprise. The consumers' cooperative, too, may become a mere retail shop with many "sleeping-partners" having a share. But in its normal development, a cooperative will follow a different path. When the leading principle is the will of the consumers to provide for their own needs and to become independent of trade and of its distributory advantages, in other words, when the cooperators pursue the goal of self-production with decisiveness, energy, and intelligence, then the development is normal. Cooperative self-production, however, must also be carried out in the same manner as the production by other owners of capital and other entrepreneurs. Cooperatives, too, must use wage labor, and as long as the laborers feel that *even such* capital is an alien or even hostile power, then—subjectively and apparently—nothing has changed for the laborers of such enterprises.

The question is, do they have reason, are they *entitled* to feel and think this way? The question must be answered in the *negative,* the more so, the more the workers are or become cooperators themselves, and thus the more they *participate* in the enterprise and in its objectives. They benefit for themselves and for their families of the advantages and the *blessings* of the cooperative movement. But, what is perhaps even more important, they can also anticipate and actively work for the advantages which their children and grandchildren will have within the cooperative movement. For, this is the most important issue: to create a foundation capital which will be of benefit to future generations.

He who has no appreciation for this, who is only able to dully and stupidly consider the *momentary* advantage, will feel "exploited" by the cooperative, even when he is a cooperator himself, when, for example, he works as a laborer in a cooperative factory, or as a salesman in a cooperative store or in a wholesale cooperative. This is a question of judgment and insight, but judgment and insight are here, as in so many other instances, dependent on moral maturity and on *good will*. But good will in this sense is not the heroic will of self-conquest, of sacrifice in its most sublime manifestations. It only asks for insight into the well apprehensible, the deeply understood interest that we all have, the interest to care for the *future*. This interest will change almost imperceptibly from a very real into a very ideal one, and the more it becomes ideal, the more it is transformed into a matter of strong conviction; in this rests the genuine cooperative *spirit*.

7. The greatest weakness of Marx's system of thought is the disregard of moral power, of moral will. This disregard is an inherent trait of his system. Although *Capital* and other writings abound with moral indignation, vigorous accusations against hardheartedness, shamelessness, greed, against merciless vandalism, against the most infamous, dirtiest, and meanest hateful passions, although Marx is hearing the monotonous song of the furies of private interest everywhere, he plainly refuses to appeal to the moral consciousness of the laborer, much less to that of the capitalist, in order to improve or even to abolish those conditions which he depicts in such crass colors and which he occasionally compares to the head of Medusa or to other monsters.

He speaks of the "great duty" of the proletariat only in terms of their conquest of political power and also of their duty to fathom the secrets of international politics. He also commends the heroic resistance of labor groups during strikes and lockouts. In practical matters the moral pathos never deserted him. Also, in his personal and family life, in interaction with friends, as a human being in general, he was undoubtedly full of morally strong sentiments which sometimes even showed a certain severity and harshness, as when he condemned the mistakes and shortcomings of others, such as Lassalle. And often enough he was chiding the "riff-raff" *(Lumpenpack)* in circles especially close to him.

The exclusion of moral sentiments from the premises of socialism or of any other social reform is a purely theoretical, or better, a doctrinal matter. It is based on the assiduity to formulate pure theory. Such theory, his own doctrine, is considered to be free of any such motivational causes; they are not needed and are therefore rejected. On the one hand, this theory confides in the process, as such, and in the natural drives, the instincts which are revealed therein. These are the instincts of conflict and of the class-conflict—the decision is supposed to be right here, now as in earlier times. On the other hand, the theory relies on rational, clear cognition not of that which should be, but of that which is.

Undoubtedly Marx was right when he said (in a letter to Sorge, October 18, 1877) that the "materialistic basis," i.e., the economic development, would need to be studied seriously and objectively if actions were to be grounded on it. He was right when he thought that the revolutionary empty talk of a German named Most was ridiculous and when he thought that the recent utopianist "game of fantasy" on the future structure of society was a foolish and basically reactionary affair. He also realized the danger of a righteous fanaticism and of unpolitical behavior which almost regularly go together with vigorless vanity and sentimental sensuality. Marx, however, failed to recognize that there is a kind of moral idealism of quite a different nature, one that he was wrong to banish from his considerations. He ignored that political power, like any other power, turns against itself; that it brings misery to its opponents unless it unites wisdom and prudence with the sense of justice. He ignored the fact that moral reasoning, for and against the existing order, for and against laws and rights, will always have the most enduring and lasting effects on the consciousness of the educated people, as well as on the generally naive consciousness of the common people, because moral reasoning is always the most convincing kind of reasoning. This is true even though moral reasoning may originate in inherited or otherwise transmitted prejudice of the individual who may not even be aware of these origins which, in their turn, may have their roots in the individual's personal or class interests.

8. The truth of the basic idea of the "materialistic" conception of history is so evident that, whenever it is correctly understood, it may be used as a leading thread for study even by

other thinkers than Marx and Engels or their followers. This is
true because the general life of the people *(Volksleben)* must
necessarily and continuously influence the formation of the
political and intellectual life, because the latter two rest upon
the former and are unthinkable without it. Although the general life of the people is in part also determined by politics and
intellectual life, it is yet relatively independent of both, at least
in its most essential aspects and processes. This is so because
the life of the people is ruled merely by elementary drives and
motives which govern the social life as such, like the vegetative
life in the organism of the mammal which is relatively independent of the motor and sensory organs. But this general
social life is economic life. Although customs, law, and governmental power are conditioning it in all its spheres, the economic life has needs to which these forces are directed, from
which they were originally derived. The same is true for the
intellectual life; but besides and beyond the material needs
there are also intellectual needs, even though they are rooted
in the material needs, as for example the need for adornments
in sexual life, the need for religion in all crises of individual and
social life, and the need for art which is rooted again in the
need for religion, for adornment, and in elementary needs.

The proposition that man's consciousness is determined by
man's existence as a social being and not vice versa has to be
altered to read that consciousness is more strongly and more
directly determined by man's existence as such *(das Sein)*.
Moves and changes within "existence"—although they may be
in part caused by moves and changes within consciousness—
are, nevertheless, determined in a most decisive manner by
their own inherent causality. Although moves and changes
within consciousness may also have an own inherent causality,
they are yet, above all, dependent on the changes within existence and may therefore, to a large extent, be interpreted as
functions (in a mathematical sense) of the latter.

Marx is also correct in asserting that it is in conflicts and
crises of social life that these influences become decisive and
historically relevant. But this is so precisely because the forms
of consciousness, because law and *because* the ways of thinking
also have their own inner causality and above all, *because* their

inertness is extremely high. The class-conflicts and revolutions are—according to Marx—subjective expressions of such objective contradictions. However, Marx does not realize the fact that such contradictions may at he same time signify the death of a culture, of the "Gemeinschaft"-like life of the folk. He ignores that such contradictions are basically unsolvable and incurable. Although there may be a simultaneous development of a younger culture from the older, there is, nevertheless, no necessity for such a development. The essential condition for such a development is not the victorious progress of new productive powers, of a new technology, and the dictatorship of a class, but the ascent of new human beings, of new peoples and of the winning of new land for them—as far as we are at all entitled to draw conclusions from the past and project them onto the future.

Marx's absolute certainty about the decline of the present and the rise of the future form of society does not stand the test of experience. The analogy of the transition from the feudal to the capitalistic order of society is no proof at all. This analogy was already the basic theme of the *Communist Manifesto*. As early as 1847 Marx believed he perceived that for decades the history of industry and trade had been nothing but a history of the rebellion of the modern powers of production against the modern conditions of production and against the distribution of property, which represent the conditions of life of the bourgeoisie and of its rule—the commercial crises are considered as proof for this. He constructed the following parallel from the past: "The means of production and of exchange, on whose foundation the bourgeoisie built itself up, were generated in feudal society. At a certain stage in the development of these means of production and of exchange, the conditions under which feudal society produced and exchanged and the feudal organization of agriculture and manufacturing industry, in one word, the feudal relations of property, became no longer compatible with the already developed productive forces; they became so many fetters. They had to be burst asunder; they were burst asunder."[18]

Marx and Engels were absolutely convinced that this analogy was correct and that the conclusions would permit forecasting the coming development; their conviction led them to expect the outbreak of the proletarian revolution with each commercial crisis they lived to experience. But even if the analogy were correct, this would by no means necessitate the final "dissolution" of classes, the end of the "ultimate" antagonistic form of the social production process as a result of the proletarian revolution. Marx's prediction that the passing of this present form of society would "therefore" put an end to the prehistory of human society, is a prophecy out of the blue. At this point Marx becomes a visionary; he shows a kind of utopian confidence which has more resemblance to religious faith than to scientific thought. Marx envisions the consummation of the material foundations on which the more advanced form of society will rest. The basic principle of this higher form of society is for him the complete and free development of every individual.

For the above reasons, Marx is following Owen's suggestions in considering the factory system as representing the germ cell for the education in the future, which will consist of a combination of productive work and theoretical instruction and sports for all children beyond a certain age. This educational method is not only intended to increase social production, but is considered to be the only method to produce well-rounded human beings.[19] This human being of the future should be able to fulfill various kinds of social functions in consecutive activities; the former division of labor would be abolished forever. "Moreover, it is obvious that the fact of the collective working group, being composed of individuals of both sexes and all ages, must necessarily, under suitable conditions, become a source of *human development;* although in its spontaneously developed, brutal capitalistic form . . . that fact is a pestiferous source of corruption and slavery."[20]

9. Even persons who do not share this confidence in the future and who think that the belief in the coming of a classless, as well as a competition-less and conflict-free society is an illusion, will find themselves sympathetically impressed by those ideas.[21] But why is it that Marx not only desires, but even predicts and confides in a humane development, and yet restrains the socialist workers from also striving for this high

moral goal; why does he restrain them from being motivated by the hope and the desire for a more genuine humanity? We know why: Marx was afraid that the revolutionary spirit might weaken and diminish; although he abhorred fanaticism and revolutionary empty talk. Did he not desire that the revolutionary process take place within "more humane" paths? Was it not his idea that these more humane paths were dependent on the stage of evolution of the proletariat? Does a higher stage of evolution not include the faith in moral ideals, the enthusiasm for them? Obviously, Marx is seriously wrong when he—even in the case that his theory of the relationship between existence *(Sein)* and consciousness were correct—wants to dictate to the proletariat the ways and forms in which they, the workers, should fight out the conflict between productive powers and property relations. He is wrong when he seems to restrain the proletariat from developing a moral, humane consciousness.

Marx has often been accused of having excluded his own theory from the idea of scientific truth and of general validity by claiming that in its essential contents, his theory merely represents an expression of class consciousness, a weapon within the class war. This would imply that in fact there is no true and valid political economy, but that there is only the economics of capital on the one hand and that of labor on the other. It is true that Marx himself was in part responsible for much of the "ideological plaster" that is covering his economic theory. He often lacks the objectivity and impartiality of genuine theoretical thinking. Moreover, he could not really expect that more than one or two out of a hundred normally class-conscious workers would be able to understand his theoretical work. But every normal human being has a *moral consciousness*, although it may often prove to be poorly developed or hidden under a veil of religiousness and thereby not accessible to cognition. And this moral consciousness is a weapon all the stronger the more it is directed against unjust circumstances, against the horrors of civilization, against the humiliations of humanity, and where it fights for better conditions of life for man. For, these ideals are not bound to one class, they much rather depend upon the natural, inborn disposition of the heart and of the character, upon the spiritual atmosphere in which a person grows up, upon the influence of educators and teachers, of things read and heard, of empathy and knowledge —in short, upon the whole moral education. On this, they depend much more than upon the consciousness of one's own misery, the indignation about it, and about the sad condition of one's fellowmen. This is true even though insurgent movements, carrying in themselves little chance for changes for the better, are more likely to arise directly from such misery, and often have a temporary beneficial effect due to the elementary energy with which such movements tend to expose the misery. However, with respect to lasting effects, theoretical groundings, and practical-political consequences, the proletarian movements in all countries have not been started and led by members of the proletariat, but—to a smaller or larger extent —by persons who, because of their family background and education, were members of other classes. Marx and Engels are outstanding examples of this.

Despite the deficiencies inherent in his work and deed, it is, above all, Marx who will maintain his rank as an epoch-making man and thinker throughout the centuries to come, uniting infinite light with his own light.

NOTES AND REFERENCES

1. T.N.: Cap. I 363.
2. T.N.: Ibid.
3. *Theorien über den Mehrwert,* 3 vols., ed. by K. Kautsky, vol. II, p. 564.
4. T.N.: Ibid.
5. T.N.: Cap. III 370. For reference to Karl Marx's third volume of *Capital* here and below, the following publication detail is relevant: vol. III (Moscow: Foreign Languages Publishing House, 1962).
6. T.N.: Theorien II 507.
7. Cap. I 364. T.N.: He states (in Theorien III 565) that a part of the labor of leadership arises only from the hostile antagonism between capitalist and laborer and belongs to the *faux frais de production.*
8. T.N.: Cap. I 187.
9. T.N.: Ibid., pp. 835–83.
10. T.N.: Ibid., p. 365.
11. T.N.: Ibid.
12. T.N.: Cap. III 320.
13. T.N.: Ibid., p. 324.
14. T.N.: Ibid.
15. T.N.: Ibid., p. 325. The formula M-C-M' means that M (or money) is exchanged for C (or commodity) resulting in M' (or money plus surplus value; i.e., profit upon alienation).
16. T.N.: Cap. I 834.
17. T.N.: Cap. III 331.
18. T.N.: S W I 39.
19. T.N.: Cap. I 529.
20. T.N.: Ibid., p. 536.
21. Recently Staudinger has succinctly summarized ("Konsumgenossen-schaftliche Bundschau," 31, VII, 1920) his analysis of class struggles and competition in the sentence that I cited on the back side of the dedication [p. xvii of this edition]. Sombart also criticised the theory in the same line of thought.

Index of Names

Subject Index

Accumulation: of capital, 101–2, 104–5, 112; role of state in, 105, 106; stepwise development of, 102

Agriculture, 98, 104

Alienation, 155–56

Alsace-Lorraine, 73

Augsburger Allgemeine, 6, 7

Bourgeoisie, 25, 27–28: English, 20, 36; French, 41, 45, 48, 51; German, 4, 21; state and society of, 12, 20, 21, 26, 29, 31, 39; and struggle with proletariat, 31, 37, 38

Capital, 16, 38–39, 44; accumulation of, 101–2, 104–5, 112; centralization of, 103, 112; constant, 101, 102; and credit, 103; and industrial, 106; and labor, 95, 104; and market expansion, 112; and money, 87–88; organic composition of, 102; and production, 87, 101, 102, 109; and surplus value, 112; variable, 101, 102, 109

Capital (Das Kapital), 3, 30, 53, 57, 68, 71, 85–107

Capitalism, viii, ix, x; development of, in colonies, 105–6; essence of, 151–54; Marx's hatred of, x, 81; production mode of, 20, 29, 31, 36, 37, 38, 89–90, 93, 95, 96, 100–1, 117–18

Chartism and Chartists, 23, 29, 30, 31, 33, 34, 36, 45, 54, 56, 67

Christianity, 12, 13

Civil War, U.S., 62, 63

Classes: abolition of, 139; bourgeois, 27, 39; social, 11, 29, 37, 49. *See also* Bourgeoisie; Proletariat.

Class struggle, 27, 29, 37, 40, 52, 120, 124, 128, 162

Colonies and capitalism, 105–6

Commune, Paris, 74, 75, 82

Communism, 7, 8, 9, 22, 24, 27, 28, 32–45

Communist League, 31, 58, 59, 63

Communist Manifesto, 32, 37, 38, 40, 41, 45, 66, 78, 139, 159

Communist Union, 41

Competition, 16, 17, 27, 39, 85, 90, 109

Condition of the Working Class in England, The, 24, 25, 30, 36

Conflict, ix, 17, 27, 112; class, 120; of exploiter and exploited, 90; and labor and capital, 95, 104; progress resulting from, 27, 29; and supply and demand, 110. *See also* Class struggle.

Conflict theory, viii, 27, 45; Marx's advocacy of, 47, 158; Tönnies response to, 158, 159

Contraditions: of capitalistic mode of production, 124; between labor and machine inputs, 94; in Marx's writings, 147; between wages and profits, 120; between wealth and poverty, 16–17

"Contribution to the Critique of Hegel's Philosophy of Right," 10

Cooperatives, 66, 126, 155–56

Cottage industry, 96

Crime, 17

Crises, economic, 16, 65, 96, 112, 125

Critique of the Political Economy, 59, 60, 85–107

Democracy, 36, 62

Depressions. *See* Crises, economic.

Dialectical method, ix, 61, 122–23

AI